State
Air Pollution
Control Laws

**by
Stanley E. Degler**

BNA's Environmental Management Series

184464

Printed in the United States of America

Library of Congress Catalog Card Number: 79-77350

TABLE OF CONTENTS

State Air Pollution Control Laws

As recently as 1963, only 14 states had laws providing for air pollution control on a statewide basis, while two others had limited-coverage laws.

Under the impetus of federal legislation aiding state programs, 46 states now have such laws, although some still have too limited coverage to meet the requirements of the federal Clean Air Act of 1967.

Most of this state legislation was enacted in 1967. Forty-eight states had legislative sessions that year and 39 of these considered air pollution control bills. Twenty legislatures enacted comprehensive air pollution control laws, and six others adopted amendments to strengthen existing legislation.

With minor variations, the procedures for developing and promulgating regulations for air pollution control are similar in most states. Usually, the control-agency staff drafts the proposed regulations, with either formal or informal assistance or review by outside technical experts and affected interests. Then formal hearings are held, followed by official action by a state board or commission.

Federal officials report that some states have not been vigorous in implementing their control authority, however. In his 1968 report on the Clean Air Act, the Secretary of Health, Education, and Welfare said that "they have failed to adopt emission standards or ambient air quality standards as part of their regulatory activities." But he added that there is some recent evidence of improvement, especially in the newer state programs.

Twenty states have adopted emission standards, as compared with 14 a year earlier and seven in 1963. Other states currently are in the process of formulating standards.

State resources devoted to air pollution control also have increased greatly during the last few years. Before the Clean Air Act, the total annual allocation for state air pollution control programs amounted to a little over $3-million. California alone accounted for more than half the total, with New York and New Jersey having the only other programs with budgets over $100,000. Now, total annual budgets have more than tripled, and 22 states have programs with spending exceeding $100,000.

About half the states also have legislation exempting industrial pollution control facilities from taxes of one sort or another.

This book contains a summary of the status of the law on air pollution control in each state, the District of Columbia, Puerto Rico, and the cities of Chicago, Detroit, New York, Philadelphia, and Pittsburgh. The states without general air pollution laws are Alabama, Maine, Nebraska, North Dakota, and South Dakota. These states do have laws on the abatement of nuisances which may be applied to air pollution.

The entire text of the California statute is reproduced, by way of example, because California has the most advanced program of air pollution control of any state. The California law was extensively amended in 1968, with the motor vehicle pollution control sections completely rewritten. Massachusetts, Vermont and Puerto Rico adopted new laws in 1968, as did Congress for the District of Columbia.

The text of suggested state legislation developed by the Council of State Governments also is reproduced. Many of the state statutes have been based on this model law.

STATE AIR POLLUTION CONTROL LEGISLATION

	Control	Local Option	Tax Incentives	Regulations
Alabama				
Alaska	X			X
Arizona	X*	X		
Arkansas	X			X
California	X	X	X	X
Colorado	X	X		
Connecticut	X	X	X	X
Delaware	X			X
District of Columbia	X			
Florida	X	X	X	X
Georgia	X	X	X	X
Hawaii	X	X		X
Idaho	X	X	X	
Illinois	X	X	X	X
Indiana	X	X	X	
Iowa	X	X		X
Kansas	X	X		

STATE AIR POLLUTION CONTROL LEGISLATION—Contd.

	Control	Local Option	Tax Incentives	Regulations
Kentucky	X	X		X
Louisiana	X			X
Maine				
Maryland	X	X		X
Massachusetts	X	X	X	X
Michigan	X	X	X	X
Minnesota	X	X	X	
Mississippi	X	X		
Missouri	X	X		X
Montana	X	X	X	
Nebraska		X		
Nevada	X	X		
New Hampshire	X		X	X
New Jersey	X	X	X	X
New Mexico	X	X		
New York	X	X	X	X
North Carolina	X	X	X	
North Dakota	X.*			
Ohio	X	X	X	
Oklahoma	X	X		
Oregon	X	X	X	X
Pennsylvania	X	X		X
Rhode Island	X		X	X
South Carolina	X	X	X	X
South Dakota				
Tennessee	X	X		
Texas	X	X		X
Utah	X	X		
Vermont	X			
Virginia	X	X		X
Washington	X	X	X	
West Virginia	X	X	X	X
Wisconsin	X	X	X	
Wyoming	X		X	X
Puerto Rico	X			
Virgin Islands	X			

*Limited coverage under general health provisions.

ABILITY OF STATES TO FUNCTION UNDER AIR QUALITY ACT OF 1967 ACCORDING TO THEIR AIR POLLUTION CONTROL LAWS

State	Authority to Divide States into Territories	Emergency Action Provision	Authority to Set Air Quality Standards	Authority to Set Emission Standards	Enforcement P = Permits F = Fines I = Inspection C = Criminal (Misd.) Inj = Injunctive O = Orders	Notes
Alabama	—		—	—	—	—
Alaska	?	O	X	App.	P, F, I, C, Inj, O	—
Arizona	O	O	?	?	I, Inj, O	—
Arkansas	X	O	X	App.	P, I, C, Inj(?),O	—
California	X	O	X	X	Inj, O, C	—
Colorado	X	X	X*	X*	F, I, Inj, O, C	*Air Quality and Emission Standards in Statute
Connecticut	X	X	App.	App.	F, I, Inj, O	—
Delaware	X	X	App.	App.	F, I, Inj, O, P	—
D. of Columbia	O	X	X	X	F, C, O, Inj	—
Florida	X	X	X	App.	P, F, I, Inj, O, C*	*Misdemeanor for violation of orders only
Georgia	X	X	X	X	I, O, C	—
Guam	—	—	—	—	—	—
Hawaii	X	O	X	App.	P, F, I, Inj, O	—
Idaho	X*	O	App.	App.	F, I, Inj, O	*States Commission may organize a county air pollution control division-Implying one or more counties could be segregated.
Illinois	X	O	App.	App.	F, I, Inj, O, P	Consistent local programs may be exempted
Indiana	O	O	App.	App. Ltd.	I, O	Primarily a local government program.

ABILITY OF STATES TO FUNCTION UNDER AIR QUALITY ACT OF 1967 ACCORDING TO THEIR AIR POLLUTION CONTROL LAWS—Contd.

State	Authority to Divide States into Territories	Emergency Action Provision	Authority to Set Air Quality Standards	Authority to Set Emission Standards	Enforcement P = Permits F = Fines I = Inspection C = Criminal (Misd.) Inj = Injunctive O = Orders	Notes
Iowa	X	X	X	X	F, I, Inj, O, P	Consistent local programs may be exempted.
Kansas	X	X	X	X	F, I, Inj, O, P	—
Kentucky	App.	X	X	X	P, F, I, C, O	Consistent local programs may be exempted.
Louisiana	X	O	App.	App.	F, I, Inj, O	—
Maine	—	—	—	—	—	—
Maryland	X	X	X	X	F, O	—
Massachusetts	X	O	App.	App.	F, I, Inj, O	—
Michigan	X	X	App.	App.	F, I, Inj, O	—
Minnesota	X	O	X	X	F, Inj, C	—
Mississippi	?	X	X	X	P, F, I, C, O, Inj	—
Missouri	X	X	X	X	F, I, Inj, O	Consistent local programs may be exempted
Montana	X	X	X	X	P, C, I, F, O, Inj	—
Nebraska	—	—	—	—	—	—
Nevada	?	—	App.	App.	O, Inj, I, C	Primarily a county and district operation.
New Hampshire	?	X	App.	App.	I, O, Inj, F	—
New Jersey	?	X	App.	App.	P, I, Inj, F	—
New Mexico	X	X	App.	X	Inj, (also local penalties)	Local programs may elect to be exempted
New York	X	X	X	X	I, F, Inj, O	—
North Carolina	App.	X	X	X	P, O, I, C, F, Inj	—

ABILITY OF STATES TO FUNCTION UNDER AIR QUALITY ACT OF 1967 ACCORDING TO THEIR AIR POLLUTION CONTROL LAWS—Contd.

State	Authority to Divide States into Territories	Emergency Action Provision	Authority to Set Air Quality Standards	Authority to Set Emission Standards	Enforcement P = Permits F = Fines I = Inspection C = Criminal (Misd.) Inj = Injunctive O = Orders	Notes
North Dakota	—	—	—	—	—	—
Ohio	X	O	X	X	I, P, F, Inj, C(?)	—
Oklahoma	X	O	App.	X	C	—
Oregon	X	X	X	X	I, Inj, C	Authorizes regional programs also
Pennsylvania	X	O	App.	X	C, F, Inj	Can set up regional authority
Puerto Rico	—	—	—	—	—	—
Rhode Island	X	X	X	App.	I, P, O, Inj, C, F	—
South Carolina	O	O	App.	App.	F, Inj, O, P, I, C	—
South Dakota	—	—	—	—	—	—
Tennessee	?	X	X	X	P, I, O, Inj, C	—
Texas	X	O	App.	App.	I, O, Inj, F	—
Utah	X	O	X	X	I, O, C, Inj, F	—
Vermont	X	X	X	X	F, I, O	—
Virginia	X	O	App.	App.	I, F, Inj(?)	—
Virgin Islands	X	X	App.	X	I, P, C,, Inj	—
Washington	X	X	X (goal)	X	O, Inj, F, I	—
West Virginia	?	X	?	App.	O, I, Inj, F	—
Wisconsin	?(Classified 144.38)	X	?	?	O, I	—

X = Yes } Specific, Clear
O = No }
App = Apparent
? = Uncertain

Alabama

Current authority is limited to general nuisance provisions of existing state statutes. Thus, while municipal programs have no specific enabling legislation, the rights and duties of municipalities with regard to public health regulations have been upheld in many cases. It should be noted that county and metropolitan agencies lack specific control authority.

No standards or regulations have been adopted by the state.

Air pollution legislation was considered by the 1967 legislature but failed to pass. The next regular session of the legislature is in 1969.

(Sections 75 and 76, Code of Alabama, Recompiled 1958, Title 22.)

Alaska

While there is no specific reference to atmospheric pollution in the enumeration of powers of the Board of Health, power to regulate atmospheric pollution is derived from a 1951 statute which provides that the Board of Health is empowered, directed, and authorized to adopt rules and regulations for "regulation of sanitation and sanitary practices in the interest of public health." The 1959 Alaska Air Pollution Code empowered the Commissioner of Health and Welfare to abate and prevent air pollution by adopting and enforcing allowable air quality standards. Violation of the regulation is a misdemeanor and is punishable by fine or imprisonment.

(Alaska Compiled Laws Annotated 1949, Sections 40-1-6(b), (c), as amended, Chapter 56, Laws 1951, Section 1; Air Pollution Code adopted by Board of Health effective on or before July 28, 1959.)

Arizona

Arizona adopted an act, effective in 1967, which provides for the establishment of a Division of Air Pollution Control in the state Department of Health, empowers the Board of Health to adopt rules and regulations, and empowers the Division of Air Pollution Control to enforce such rules and regulations. Provisions of the law relating to air pollution control are applicable to all lands within the state, including Indian tribal lands. Provisions include methods of control pertaining to motor vehicles and vehicle emission control devices and establishment of an advisory council.

The board of supervisors of each county may adopt rules and regulations to correct, remove, or prevent air pollution in all its forms except emissions from motor vehicles and may authorize or designate an existing department of the county government or establish an air pollution control district to carry out necessary investigations, inspections, and enforcement of such rules and regulations. The act provides the state and counties with injunctive powers and provides fines for those found to be in contempt of an injunctive order of a court.

No standards or regulations have been adopted by the state, although open burning was prohibited by the 1967 act (with some minor exceptions).

(Arizona Revised Statutes Annotated, Air Pollution, Chapter 6, Article 8, 36-771 to 36-790; Chapter 14, Article 1, 36-1701 to 36-1719; Motor Vehicles, Chapter 3, Article 1, 28-327, and Chapter 6, Article 16, 28-955.)

Arkansas

In 1965 the name of the Water Pollution Control Commission was changed to Arkansas Pollution Control Commission and given new powers to control air pollution. The Commission is empowered to adopt rules and regulations, hold hearings, enter orders, and represent the state in interstate compacts. The act is the exclusive means within the state for the control of air pollution.

The commission has issued a proposed air pollution control code covering open burning and pollutants in general.

(Section 82-1901 et seq., Arkansas Statutes.)

California

In 1947 the State Department of Health was deemed responsible for certain duties with respect to air pollution control work within the state. These duties include special studies, establishment of air quality and motor vehicle standards, air monitoring, and assistance to local agencies. In 1960 authority for motor vehicle emission control was vested in the Motor Vehicle Pollution Control Board (for certification of control devices), the Bureau of Motor Vehicles (for enforcement of control device installation), and the Highway Patrol (for inspection and certification of installation stations). The responsibility for enforcement of air pollution control regulations on stationary sources was vested in the county air pollution control districts.

In general the 1967 Act:

• Abolishes the Motor Vehicle Pollution Control Board and creates a State Air Resources Board, prescribing its organization, powers, duties, and functions to coordinate administration, research, and the establishment of standards for air conservation activities within the state;

• Requires all facilities, including funds, records, equipment, and personnel of the Motor Vehicle Pollution Control Board and of the State Vehicular Pollution Laboratory of the State Department of Public Health in Los Angeles, over which the Department has control to be transferred to the State Air Resources Board;

• Provides for division of the state into basins having similar geographical and meteorological conditions by January 1, 1969, and authorizes, but does not require, the formation of county air pollution control or regional districts in areas where existing districts are not functioning; prohibits more than one regional air pollution control district in any basin;

• Permits local or regional authority to adopt standards and rules and regulations more restrictive than those of the State Air Resources Board; declares that air resources provisions shall not be deemed to affect existing rules and regulations of a district until the State Air Resources Board has reviewed such rules and regulations;

• Requires, with certain exceptions, that the Board enforce its standards and rules and regulations within areas under the jurisdiction of a local or regional authority, if such local or regional authority does not comply with a directive from the Board where the Board has determined that its standards are not being complied with, or are inadequate, and the reply of the local or regional authority to a request from the Board for a report on the matter is unsatisfactory; vests in the Board power to take any appropriate legal action to carry out its responsibilities in such area, as well as authority to take any action which an air pollution control district could take;

• Makes a misdemeanor of any violation of standards and rules and regulations prescribed by the Board in any area in which the Board is enforcing such standards and rules and regulations;

• Exempts the Bay Area Pollution Control District and Humboldt County from the provisions relating to regional districts but requires the Bay Area District to file its rules and regulations with the State Air Resources Board;

• Deletes provisions requiring the Department of Public Health to maintain a program of air sanitation but requires the department to submit to the State Air Resources Board recommendations for ambient air quality standards and requires that standards adopted by the Board relating to health effects be based upon such recommendations;

• Distinguishes and defines vehicular and nonvehicular sources of air pollution.

The state law was amended in 1968 by the California Pure Air Act, which related primarily to motor vehicles.

The Air Resources Board adopted regulations under the act, including those for standard and test procedures for motor vehicles, on June 18, 1968. The Board currently is considering division of the state into nine air basins and plans to set air quality standards for each in 1969.

(Health and Safety Code of the State of California, Division 1, Part 1, Chapter 2, Article 9, and Division 26.)

Colorado

The Colorado Air Pollution Control Act was enacted in 1966 and amended in 1967. This act provides for ambient air standards for the state and emission standards in designated basins, and also permits local authorities to enact laws consistent with or more restrictive than the state act. The act creates an air pollution variance board as a division of the Public Health Department. The Department of Health is empowered to enforce compliance with emission standards. Provisions of the act provide injunctive powers and penalties.

State ambient air standards exist for suspended particulates, coefficient of haze, total oxidants, oxides of nitrogen, and sulfur dioxide. Emission standards in designated areas regulating smoke, open burning, particulates, and gases are included in the act.

Stronger state legislation will be considered by the 1969 legislature. The Department has announced it will propose major revisions to enable Colorado to meet requirements of the federal Air Quality Act.

(Chapter 45, pp. 210-226, Laws 1966 as amended by SB 380 approved June 8, 1967.)

Connecticut

The Connecticut Air Pollution Control Law was approved July 7, 1967. It created an air pollution control commission authorized to promulgate regulations on a statewide or regional basis, to hold hearings as to air pollution upon complaints received or upon the commission's own initiative, and to sue for injunctive enforcement of commission orders and regulations and for penalties. The Commissioner of Health is given the executive authority to carry out the commission's program.

Summary abatement provisions for pollution emergencies are provided as well as a procedure for variances.

Individual or joint action by local governmental bodies is permitted if the ordinances so promulgated conform to the state air pollution regulations. State regulations covering emergencies have been adopted.

(Public Act 754, Laws 1967.)

Delaware

The Delaware Air and Water Resources Commission, created by state legislation in 1966, is authorized to promulgate rules and regulations, issue orders, develop a comprehensive program for the prevention and control of air pollution, cooperate with other control groups, conduct studies, make investigations, and hold hearings. Violations are punishable by fine.

Regulations covering refuse disposal, smoke, particulates, and sulfur dioxide have been adopted by the state. Proceedings to abate nuisances may be instituted in the name of the state or on behalf of the Commission.

(Water and Air Resources Act, 1966, Chapter 442, Volume 55, Laws of Delaware.)

District of Columbia

Congress in 1968 adopted the District of Columbia Air Pollution Control Act.

The District of Columbia Council was given power to enact regulations to control emissions from fuel combustion at stationary sources, emissions from solid waste disposal and salvage operations, visible emissions, process emissions, and motor vehicle emissions. The regulations must be at least as stringent as the recommendations of the Secretary of Health, Education, and Welfare in the Washington-area air pollution abatement enforcement conference.

(PL 90-440.)

Florida

The 1957 Florida Air Pollution Control Act established an Air and Water Pollution Control Commission and provided for establishment of air pollution control districts for state enforcement of the Commission's air pollution control rules and regulations in such districts. The Commission has the power to formulate, adopt, promulgate, amend, and repeal rules and regulations. Local governmental authorities may adopt regulations and standards provided they are not in conflict with or less stringent than established state regulations and standards. The state also has provided some specific legislation giving certain counties control authority. The statute was amended in 1967.

Standards regulating visible smoke, particulate matter, fluorides, and power plant emissions have been adopted. In addition, a permit system covering both new and existing installations has been adopted.

(Chapter 403, Florida Air and Water Pollution Control Act; SB 520, Laws of Florida, 1967.)

Georgia

The Georgia State Code, relating to Air Quality Control, was amended in 1967. The Board of Health is empowered to adopt, modify, repeal, and promulgate rules and regulations after due notice and public hearings, and to exercise general supervision of the administration and enforcement of the act and all rules, regulations, and orders promulgated thereunder. The Department of Public Health is charged with administration and enforcement of the act and all rules, regulations, and orders promulgated thereunder. Violation of any provision is punishable as a misdemeanor.

Regulations were adopted by the state in 1968 covering smoke, particulates, fluorides, sulfur dioxide, other chemicals, and open burning.

(Georgia Code Chapter 88-9.)

Hawaii

Hawaii's "Air Pollution Control Act" of 1957 established a statewide program of air pollution control under the Department of Health. The department may formulate and promulgate, amend, and repeal rules and regulations controlling and prohibiting air pollution within the state or within specific areas of the state. Provisions allow the department to organize a county advisory air pollution control association in any county and require the department to submit all rules and regulations of strictly local application to the appropriate county association before adoption. The act provides for injunctive powers and fine. County air pollution control agencies may adopt and enforce rules and regulations, provided they are not inconsistent with the act.

Standards and regulations have been adopted for the Islands of Oahu (1958), Maui (1965), and Kauai (1966). Agricultural operations and several other minor air pollution sources were exempted from the control provisions of the regulations. The Oahu regulations include provisions to establish a source registration system and to control smoke, dust, soot, and fumes. The Maui and Kauai regulations include provisions to establish a source registration system and to control smoke, dust, particulate matter, soot and fumes, sulfur dioxides, open fires, incinerators and disposal equipment, and toxic chemicals.

(Revised Laws of Hawaii 1955, As Amended, Chapter 47, Part V.)

Idaho

The Idaho Air Pollution Control Act of 1959 (and the 1967 Air Pollution Control Act of Idaho) authorized the establishment of a statewide air pollution control program and established an Air Pollution Control Commission in the State Board of Health. The Commission was empowered to adopt, after comprehensive study and survey, codes, rules, and regulations regarding air pollution, to initiate and receive complaints, to hold hearings thereon, and to institute legal proceedings and secure injunctions. The Board was empowered to require registration of air pollution sources and to police air pollution in accordance with rules and regulations adopted by the Commission.

A county air pollution control division may be organized by the Commission in each county in which the Commission determines that the establishment of such division is advisable to assist it in carrying out the purposes of the act. No ordinances or regulations of any governing body of any municipality or county or board of health not inconsistent with the act or any code, rule, or regulation adopted pursuant thereto were superseded, and nothing in the act precludes the adoption by a local agency of ordinances or regulations not inconsistent with the act or any code, rule, or regulation pursuant thereto.

Regulations are being considered by the state to take effect December 31, 1968 or early in 1969. The standards under consideration cover particulates and smoke, sulfur compounds, fluorides, miscellaneous contaminants, sampling and analytical procedures, and enforcement against violates.

(1967 Idaho Session Laws, Chapter 361.)

Illinois

In 1963 the Illinois Air Pollution Control Act was approved. The act created an Air Pollution Control Board and empowered it to prepare a plan for the proper control of air resources, to adopt and promulgate reasonable rules and regulations, and to hold hearings and enter orders as necessary to effectuate the purposes of the act. The Board represents the state in interstate compacts and negotiations. The state may issue a certificate of exemption to any political subdivision which provides for the control of air pollution, and also may revoke such a certificate. The Board may institute court action for injunctive relief and/or penalties.

Air pollution as a public nuisance is a violation of the Illinois Air Pollution Control Act. Regulations governing open burning were adopted by the state in 1965. In 1967 regulation of smoke, particulates, and a permit system were adopted. The regulations were amended in 1968, and changes affecting fertilizer plants, meat smokehouses, and asphalt batching plants, and roofing are under consideration.

(Smith-Hurd Illinois Annotated Statutes, Chapter 111-1/2, Sections 240.1 to 240.17, 1966, as amended by SB 197, Section 240.15—1967 Cumulative Annual Pocket Part.)

City of Chicago: In 1959 an Air Pollution Control Code was adopted. This Code, which was amended in 1964 and greatly strengthened in 1968, established the Department of Air Pollution Control and authorized an Air Pollution Control Committee, a Technical Advisory Board, and an Appeal Board. The Director of the Department of Air Pollution Control supervises enforcement activities, institutes necessary proceedings to prosecute violators, examines and approves air pollution control equipment plans, conducts studies, cooperates with other agencies, and makes all needed rules and regulations, with the advice and consent of the Advisory Board. Penalty provisions are provided.

Regulations to control nuisances, smoke, open burning, and particulates, and to require installation permits for certain types of equipment, are incorporated in the Air Pollution Control Code as amended in 1964.

(Air Pollution Control Ordinance, Municipal Code of Chicago.)

Indiana

The 1961 General Assembly enacted the Indiana Air Pollution Control Law to be in effect after January 1, 1963. The State Board of Health was empowered to make investigations, consider complaints and hold hearings, enter orders, adopt and promulgate reasonable rules and regulations, and bring appropriate action to enforce its final orders or determinations. The intent of the act was to support local control and responsibility; therefore, affirmative remedial action by the state is taken only in those areas where there is no local law or regulation consistent with the act, or where the local law or regulation is not being enforced adequately.

Regulations have been adopted by the state covering open burning, smoke, indirect heating, process operations, foundries, and incinerators.

(Chapter 171, Acts of 1961; codified in Title 35, Chapter 46 of Burnes Indiana Statutes, Annotated, 1965 Cumulative Pocket Part.)

Iowa

The Iowa Air Pollution Control Act, approved in 1967, created the Iowa Air Pollution Control Commission within the Department of Health. The Commission has the power to prepare comprehensive abatement plans, to promulgate regulations, to establish standards, to consider complaints, to hold public hearings, and to issue or enter such order or determination as may be necessary to carry out the act. Local control programs consistent with the act are permitted.

The commission gave preliminary approval to rules controlling open burning in August 1968.

(HB 480, Acts, 62nd General Assembly of Iowa, Regular Session, 1967.)

Kansas

An act was adopted in 1967 which provides for a coordinated statewide program of air pollution prevention, abatement, and control in Kansas. The act created a Division of Air Quality Conservation within the Department of Health and created an Air Quality Conservation Commission. The Commission was empowered to adopt, amend, and repeal rules and regulations implementing and consistent with the act and to issue orders and enforce provisions of the act.

The Department, through the Air Quality Conservation Division, was directed to provide administration of the act. Violation of a Commission order, rule, or regulation is punishable by fine, and the Commission may sue for injunction. Provisions of the act enable formulation of local air quality programs provided the Commission approves and a need for such programs is established. Local authorities having such programs may enforce Commission rules and regulations and may adopt rules and regulations not in conflict with Commission rules and regulations.

No standards or regulations have been adopted by the state. There is an ordinance covering Wyandotte County. The commission is preparing ambient air quality standards which may take effect in 1969.

(SB 428, Chapter 347 of the Laws of Kansas.)

Kentucky

In 1966 the state enacted legislation creating an Air Pollution Control Commission in the Department of Health. The Board is empowered to adopt rules and regulations, hold hearings, conduct studies, fix standards, and represent the state in negotiations. Violations of the statute are punishable by fine and may be prohibited by injunction.

A regulation on registration of air contaminants and contaminant sources has been adopted by the state. It covers incinerators, open burning, coal refuse disposal piles, and waste burners of more than two-bushel capacity. Regulations on asphalt-plant emissions and industrial processes are planned.

(Baldwin's Kentucky Revised Statutes Annotated, 1967 Cumulative Supplement, Chapter 224.)

Louisiana

The Louisiana Air Control Law of 1964 created the Air Control Commission and made the Commission the exclusive air pollution control agency in the state. The Commission was authorized to adopt rules and regulations, hold hearings, enter orders, and represent the state in the negotiation of interstate compacts. Provision was made for judicial review of Commission orders and for enforcement of final orders by injunction.

Regulation I became effective in 1965. This regulation prohibits emissions from any source that will result in "undesirable levels" over properties other than that of the person owning, leasing, renting, or controlling the operation of such source. Also prohibited is the disposal of refuse or waste material in such a manner as to cause "undesirable levels."

(Chapter 12, Title 40, Louisiana Revised Statutes, Section 2201 et seq.)

Maine

Maine established a Water and Air Environmental Improvement Commission in 1967. The commission has the power only to make studies and recommendations to the legislature. Local government units are allowed to regulate air pollution.

Statewide control authority is provided only under general nuisance provisions.

No standards or regulations have been adopted by the state.

(Title 38, Chapter 3, Revised Statutes of 1964.)

Maryland

Maryland air pollution control statutes, originally adopted in 1963 and amended in 1966, were repealed by new 1967 legislation. The 1967 legislation, effective June 1, 1967, divided the state into six "Air Quality Control Areas" and directed the Department of Health to "prepare and submit to the Board of Health for approval not later than June 1, 1968, regulations establishing standards for emissions into the air and the ambient air quality" for each of the six established areas. Statewide emission standards have been submitted, but ambient air quality standards have been delayed by the federal law.

The governing body of any local jurisdiction within any area may request the Department to recommend to the Board for adoption a regulation establishing more restrictive standards for emissions or ambient air quality to be applicable within its geographic area. The Department was directed to enforce such standards as adopted, using the facilities and services of appropriate local agencies of the jurisdictions within the areas to the maximum extent possible.

An Air Quality Control Advisory Council was established. The Board was authorized to adopt, amend, and repeal rules and regulations for the control of air pollution in the state or areas of the state and to issue orders.

Air Pollution regulations adopted by the Department provide for registration of installations and for control of pollutants in the Baltimore and Washington metropolitan areas.

(The Annotated Code of the Public General Laws of Maryland, Article 43, Sections 690-704.)

Massachusetts

The 1954 Air Pollution Control Act (as amended in 1963) authorizes the State Department of Public Health to adopt and amend rules and regulations to prevent pollution or contamination of the atmosphere, and to approve rules and regulations proposed by a local board of health or other municipal legal authority. In 1960 the Boston Metropolitan Air Pollution Control District was established, and provision was made for the formation of other districts on joint application to the Department of two or more contiguous political subdivisions. The Lower Pioneer Valley Air Pollution Control District (Springfield Metropolitan Area) was formed in 1966. Municipalities within these Districts bear the full cost of administration and enforcement, within the District, of regulations adopted and enforced by the Department. Violations of provisions of the act or rules and regulations adopted pursuant thereto are punishable by fine.

Regulations to control general nuisances, use of certain fuels, smoke, and open burning and to provide for approval of plans for large incinerators and thermal utilization units were adopted for the Boston Metropolitan District in 1961. The Department has adopted statewide regulations and has an "Air Use Management Program."

(Annotated Laws of Massachusetts, Chapter 111 and 1966 Cumulative Supplement.)

Michigan

The 1965 Michigan Air Pollution Act created the Air Pollution Control Commission within the State Department of Health. The Commission was empowered to promulgate rules and regulations for controlling or prohibiting air pollution in areas of the state affected by air pollution, and to control and abate air pollution in accordance with such rules and regulations. Violations are punishable by fine. Nothing in the act invalidates existing local laws or prevents any political subdivision from adopting laws having requirements equal to or greater than the minimum applicable requirements of state law.

Regulations adopted by the state provide for control of general nuisances, smoke, open burning, foundries, incinerators, and particulates, and for the establishment of a permit system.

(Michigan Statutes Annotated, 1965 Cumulative Supplement, as amended by Public Act No. 97, Laws 1967.)

City of Detroit: Detroit's air pollution control program was authorized under provisions of a 1947 ordinance. The program is administered by the Bureau of Air Pollution Control under the Department of Buildings and Safety Engineering, which was established by the 1918 City Charter.

The 1947 ordinance has been amended a number of times and now includes provisions for control of general nuisances, smoke, open burning, and particulates, and for an inspection and permit system.

Minnesota

The Minnesota Pollution Control Agency was created by a 1967 act. The agency is empowered to adopt regional standards of air quality, to adopt regulations, and to grant variances. Provision for enforcement by injunction was made, and penalties for violations were provided. The agency was instructed to prepare a comprehensive plan for control, abatement, or prevention of air pollution for submission to the governor and legislature by February 15, 1969. Local ordinances are permitted.

No standards or regulations have been issued.

(Minnesota Statutes 1965, as amended by Chapter 32, Laws 1967.)

Mississippi

An act was adopted in 1966 which established a State Air and Water Pollution Control Commission and authorized control, prevention, and abatement of air pollution in Mississippi. The Commission is authorized to adopt standards, rules, and regulations and to provide general supervision of administration and enforcement of provisions of the act and all rules, regulations, and orders promulgated thereunder. The Commission also is charged with operation of a permit system. Violations of provisions of the act are punishable by fine and/or imprisonment. The act, however, did not provide any additional control authority for local agencies to expand the limited general nuisance and smoke provisions applicable to municipalities.

No standards or regulations have been adopted by the state.

(Mississippi Code of 1942-Section 7106 111-136, Mississippi Laws of 1966—Chapter 258, SB 1955.)

Missouri

In 1965, the Missouri Air Conservation Law created the Air Conservation Commission. The Commission is empowered to adopt rules and regulations, hold hearings, enter orders, and represent the state in the negotiation of interstate compacts. Provision is made for an executive secretary, judicial review, and enforcement by penalties and injunctions, and for local and regional air pollution control programs.

The state has adopted air quality standards and regulations for the St. Louis Metropolitan Area. The standards cover sulfur oxides, hydrogen sulfide, oxidants, dustfall, suspended particulates, and soiling index. The regulations limit particulate matter, open burning, smoke, sulfur oxides, and odor emissions. A permit system and other provisions allow for control and prevention of air pollution. A regulation on auto exhaust emission controls took effect May 6, 1968.

(Annotated Missouri Revised Statutes, 1966 Cumulative Supplement, Chapter 203.)

Montana

The 1967 Clean Air Act of Montana provided for a coordinated statewide program of air pollution prevention, abatement, and control. The state Board of Health was empowered to adopt, amend, and repeal rules and to issue orders and enforce such orders through appropriate administrative and judicial proceedings. Violations are punishable by fine, and the Board may sue for injunction. An Air Pollution Control Advisory Council was also created. Any municipality or county may establish a local air pollution control program and may adopt and enforce ordinances or local laws that are compatible with or more stringent than those imposed by the act and rules issued thereunder.

Emission standards have been adopted covering incinerators, particulates, smoke and soot, odors, open burning, and wood waste burners. The 1967 act directed the Board of Health to establish ambient air quality standards for the state as a whole within 90 days of passage and approval of the act, and air quality standards have been adopted for 12 types of pollutants. A regulation on permits for installation of equipment also has been approved.

(Chapter 313, Laws 1967.)

Nebraska

Current authority is limited to a provision in the state statutes that enables cities having a population of 150,000 inhabitants or more to provide, by ordinance, for abatement of dense volumes of smoke.

No standards or regulations have been adopted by the state.

(Revised Statutes of Nebraska, 1943, Sections 14-102, 15-311.)

Nevada

Nevada adopted an act in 1967 that authorizes the state Department of Health and Welfare, through the state Board of Health, to promulgate, amend, and enforce reasonable rules and regulations with respect to air pollution control. The act also creates an Air Pollution Control Advisory Council, which the Board of Health must consult before promulgating or adopting rules and regulations. Authority to enforce state rules and regulations may be delegated to districts, counties, cities, or towns. Provisions of the act do not diminish or supersede powers given to districts, counties, cities, or towns to adopt and enforce laws, ordinances, rules, and regulations for air pollution control if consistent with or more restrictive than rules and regulations adopted pursuant to the act. Injunctive powers were provided by the act.

No standards or regulations have been adopted by the state.

(Chapter 445, Nevada Revised Statutes; Chapter 392, Laws of 1967.)

New Hampshire

A 1967 New Hampshire law designated the Department of Health and Welfare, Division of Public Health Services, as the state air pollution control agency. An Air Pollution Commission also was established. The commission has the power to make, issue, amend, or repeal rules and regulations for prevention, control, and abatement of air pollution. It has the power to inspect emissions, to issue orders to stop pollution, and to grant variances. It is authorized to seek court injunctions and to take emergency actions.

A regulation on open burning has been adopted.

(New Hampshire Revised Statutes Annotated as amended at Chapter 433, Laws 1967.)

New Jersey

The Air Pollution Control Act (1954), as amended and supplemented, assigns air pollution control functions to the state Department of Health. The act empowers the Department to formulate, promulgate, amend, and repeal codes and rules and regulations, to study causes, effects, and hazards of air pollution, to require registration of operations that may result in air pollution, to conduct investigations, and to receive or initiate complaints. A Clean Air Council advises the Commissioner of Health.

The code does not preclude the issuance by local agencies of regulations not inconsistent with the state code. The Department is directed to organize county air pollution control associations as needed and to enforce any rule or regulation it promulgates under the code. Violations are punishable by fine. In the event preventive or corrective measures are not taken in accordance with any order of the Department, injunctive relief may be sought.

Since 1956 the state air pollution code has provided for control and prohibition of air pollution from refuse disposal and salvage operations, smoke, combustion of solid fuel, particulates, and sulfur compounds in the form of gases, vapors, or liquid particles. The code also covers industrial process equipment, and further coverage is still under consideration.

Regulations adopted under the act place restrictions on the sulfur content of fuels.

(PL 1954. Chapter 212, Title 26:2C-1 to 2C-23, amended by PL 1962, Chapter 215, PL 1967, Chapter 105, and PL 1967, Chapter 106.)

New York

The Air Pollution Control Laws of New York State, as amended in 1966, create an Air Pollution Control Board within the Department of Health. The Board has the power and duty to formulate, adopt, and promulgate, amend, and repeal codes, rules, and regulations, to establish areas within the state, to prescribe air quality standards, emission standards, and fuel-use standards for each area, and to hold hearings and conduct investigations necessary to carry out its responsibilities under the article.

The Board also is directed to develop a general comprehensive plan to control existing and prevent new sources of air pollution, encourage voluntary control, and cooperate with other control agencies. The Commissioner of Health is authorized to enforce the codes, rules, and regulations in accordance with the policies of the Board.

Local laws, ordinances, and regulations not inconsistent with the state law are not to be superseded by the state law. The vehicle and traffic law as amended requires the installation and maintenance of vehicle emission control devices approved by the Commissioner of Health. Violations of any code, rule, or regulation are punishable by fine, and the Commissioner may request the attorney general to bring injunctive action.

In 1964 an ambient air quality objectives system was adopted for use in classifying areas of the state. The objectives are stated in terms of suspended particulates, settleable particulates, sulfur dioxide, sulfuric acid mist, beryllium, hydrogen sulfide, carbon monoxide, oxidants, fluorides (as HF in air and as F in forage), smoke, odorous substances, radioactive substances, and other toxic or deleterious substances.

Rules to prevent new air pollution were adopted in 1962. Criteria for crankcase emission controls were adopted in 1963.

Sulfur content limitations on fuels would be delayed until 1971 under rule changes on which the Board held hearings in September and October 1968. New rules on particulates also are under consideration.

(McKinney's Consolidated Laws of New York Annotated, Book 44-Public Health Law, and 1961 Cumulative Annual Pocket Part, Sections 1264 to 1299.1.)

City of New York: The Department of Air Pollution Control, headed by a Commission of Air Pollution Control, was established in 1952. The Commission has the power to regulate and control the emission into the open air of harmful or objectionable substances, to enforce all laws, rules, and regulations with respect to such emissions, and to recommend for adoption by the Board rules for the control of air pollution. The Board of Air Pollution Control was established in the Department and empowered to adopt and amend rules regulating the emission of air contaminants. Local Law 14, passed in 1966, provided for the upgrading of on-site incinerators and placed limitations on the sulfur content in fuels. The law was revised in 1968, and the control agency now is called Department of Air Resources.

The New York City Air Pollution Control Code of 1964 provides for equipment-operating permits and fuel standards. The Code also provides emission standards for smoke and open burning, visible emissions from internal combustion engines, sulfur compounds, particulate matter, and emissions of air contaminants detrimental to persons or property.

The mayor, under an executive order of November 1968, assumed sweeping powers to reduce air pollution in an emergency.

North Carolina

The North Carolina Water and Air Resources Act, adopted in 1967, created a Department of Water and Air Resources governed by a Board of Water and Air Resources.

The Board administers the act and is authorized to develop a comprehensive air pollution plan for the state, to develop and adopt air quality standards, to classify sources and require reports by operators of the sources, to develop emission control standards, and to conduct research. The Board may institute civil actions for injunctive relief. Violators may be punished by fine.

Provision is made for local air pollution control programs, subject to approval by the board of the enforcement and administration of the program and the regulations issued under it.

(Chapter 892, Laws 1967, rewriting Article 21 of Chapter 143, Volume 3C-Replacement 1964.)

North Dakota

Current authority is limited to general nuisance provisions of state statutes. A review of the present law was presented in April 1967 by a special assistant attorney general, in which he stated, "In sum, it clearly appears that the North Dakota Department of Health has the statutory authority to both directly and indirectly prevent and control air pollution by the establishment of standards of control and that injurious conditions may be abated by judicial proceedings." This opinion has not been the subject of any further action, testing, or evaluation.

Ohio

A 1967 Ohio act established an Air Pollution Control Board in the Department of Health. The Board's duties are to develop abatement programs, conduct research, adopt, modify, and repeal regulations, prescribe ambient air quality standards, prescribe emission standards for air contaminants, issue variances, require reports from polluters, monitor pollution, make inspections, and administer federal grants. There are provisions for penalties and injunctive relief. Local control programs are permitted.

(Ohio Revised Code, Sections 3704.01 to 3704.11 and 3704.99.)

Oklahoma

The Oklahoma Clean Air Act, adopted in 1967, designated the state Department of Health to administer the act, authorized the state Board of Health to promulgate rules and regulations, and created an Air Pollution Council. Violation of any provision of the act is punishable as a misdemeanor. The act does not prevent cities and towns from enacting ordinances or codes with respect to air pollution that do not conflict with provisions of the act and that contain provisions not less restrictive than those fixed by the operation of the act.

No standards or regulations have been adopted by the state. The Council held hearings in October 1968 on proposed regulations on open burning and on disabling of motor vehicle pollution control devices.

(Chapter 80, Laws 1967.)

Oregon

In 1961, the Oregon legislature enacted a comprehensive Air Pollution Control Act, to be administered by the Oregon State Sanitary Authority, providing for the control and abatement of existing pollution and the prevention of new air pollution. The Sanitary Authority was empowered to establish air quality standards and to adopt rules and regulations to control air pollution in the state or areas of the state. Violation of any rule, regulation, or final order of the Authority is a misdemeanor, and the Authority may sue for an injunction to prevent violations of specific final orders and to compel compliance. Agricultural operations, land clearing and grading, and several other minor activities are exempted from the act.

Any county or city may enact ordinances or resolutions with respect to air pollution that do not conflict with state statutes or rules and regulations promulgated thereunder. Any city or county, through its governing body, may enter into contracts and agreements with other counties and cities to establish and maintain an air pollution program and may also provide for a board or other such body for supervision, management, and operation of an air pollution control program. A Mid-Willamette Valley Air Pollution Authority has been organized.

Oregon has adopted regulations and standards for the control of smoke discharge, particle fallout rate, suspended particulate matter, chemical substances (lime dust), refuse disposal (open burning at dumps), and wigwam waste burners (used by the lumber industry).

(Oregon Revised Statutes, Sections 449.760 to 449.990.)

Pennsylvania

In 1960 the legislature enacted the Air Pollution Control Act creating, within the Department of Health, an Air Pollution Commission. The law also established Regional Air Pollution Control Associations. Thus the act provides a system for control on both state and local levels.

The Commission has the power and duty to determine and certify regions and subregions, adopt rules and regulations, hold hearings, establish maximum permissible air contaminant quantities, and require measures for minimization of air pollution. The Department of Health has the power and duty, in accordance with the policies of the Commission, to investigate sources, institute complaints, enforce compliance with Commission regulations, review plans, and inspect installation of air pollution control methods and to do whatever else is necessary and proper for effective enforcement of the act and regulations promulgated thereunder.

In each region designated by the Commission, there is an association that considers complaints and attempts to resolve them voluntarily. When voluntary resolution cannot be achieved, the complaint is referred to the Commission for action. The associations comment on and suggest local regulations. Failure to comply with regulations is unlawful and is punishable by fine, and the Commission may request the Attorney General to petition for injunctive relief.

In 1962 the Commission adopted rules and regulations that prohibit open burning, prevent and control air pollution from coal refuse disposal areas, and require approval of plans for construction of combustion equipment and of flue gas cleaning devices. In 1966, Regulation IV, which limits smoke and particulate emissions, was adopted. Other regulations cover open burning, permits, engineering guides, and laboratory procedures. Ambient air quality criteria also have been issued.

(Purdon's Pennsylvania Statutes Annotated, Title 35, Chapter 23, Sections 4001-15, 1964, as amended by HB 1456, Act No. 532, Regular Session, 1965, 1966 Cumulative Pocket Part.)

Allegheny County (Pittsburgh): In 1960, an Air Pollution Control Advisory Committee was established to study and recommend to the Board of Health appropriate means to abate air pollution, including needed additions to or revisions in the rules and regulations. The Bureau of Air Pollution Control enforces any rules and regulations, violation of which is punishable by fine or imprisonment.

In 1966 the state removed Allegheny County from its separate status and subjected the program to review by the Pennsylvania Department of Health.

Rules and regulations governing smoke and particulate emissions, open fires, and discharge radioactive materials were adopted in 1960. A permit system is provided for in the regulations.

City of Philadelphia: In 1954 the Department of Public Health was given the power and duty to investigate complaints, require proper steps to minimize created effects, hazards, or nuisances, require approval of plans, make recommendations for permits or applications, and enforce the act. The Department of Licenses and Inspections transmits to the Department of Health for its recommendations all applications, plans, and specifications relating to potential sources of air pollution and issues permits for applications acceptable to the Department of Health. The Air Pollution Control Board has the power and duty to make regulations, conduct hearings, and recommend a reasonable time for completion of a required major installation. In addition to any penalty imposed by the code, the city may apply for relief by injunction.

In 1954 a permit system was instituted for equipment installations and to limit smoke, particulates, open burning, general nuisance, and other specific emissions.

Puerto Rico

Puerto Rico adopted its "Law on the Control of Air Pollution" on June 28, 1968. The Secretary of Health of the Commonwealth is responsible for administering the law through a unit within his department. An Advisory Council on atmospheric pollution also was created, with power to make recommendations to the Secretary.

The law gives the Secretary the power to adopt, amend, and repeal regulations, to hold hearings, to issue orders and obtain compliance with them through administrative or judicial proceedings, to contract for scientific, technical, administrative, and operational services, to prepare an overall abatement plan, and to carry on information programs. Criminal penalties are provided. The law also contains emergency procedures.

(Act 157, Laws 1968, SB No. 680)

Rhode Island

In 1966 the Rhode Island Clean Air Act vested in the state Director of Health the power to develop comprehensive programs for prevention, control, and abatement of new or existing pollution, to cooperate with other control agencies, to adopt, promulgate, modify, or repeal air quality standards, to hold hearings, encourage and conduct research, issue orders, and approve plans, and to make, issue, and amend rules and regulations. Violations are punishable by fines and/or imprisonment. This law transfers the responsibility of air pollution control from local governments to the state Department of Health on a statewide basis.

Regulations adopted by the state cover coal burning, dust and fumes, open burning, and particulates.

(Chapter 256-PL of 1966.)

South Carolina

In 1965 the State Pollution Control Authority was given the responsibility of abating, controlling, and preventing air pollution.

The Authority is empowered to adopt rules and regulations, hold hearings, enter orders, represent the state in the formation of interstate compacts, and bring suit to compel compliance with its orders. Violations of Authority orders are punishable by fine, and injunctions may be imposed.

South Carolina has adopted air pollution control regulations and engineering guides. Standards prescribed by these regulations cover smoke, particulates from fuel burning installations, and sulfur dioxide emissions. New regulations have been proposed and are under consideration to cover open burning, incinerators, and total suspended particulates.

(Code of Laws of South Carolina Annotated, 1962, Title 70, Chapter 3, Sections 70-121 to 70-123, 1967 Cumulative Supplement.)

South Dakota

Current authority in state statutes is limited to general nuisance provisions.

No standards or regulations have been adopted by the state.

Tennessee

The Tennessee Air Pollution Control Act, adopted in 1967, created an Air Pollution Control Board as an independent agency.

The Board has the power and duty to prepare an abatement plan, to establish air quality standards, emission standards, and a system of permits for facilities capable of causing pollution, to promulgate rules and regulations, to make inspections, to issue orders against violators, and to institute court proceedings to compel compliance.

The jurisdiction of local air pollution control programs is not superseded, providing the locality obtains a certificate of exemption by May 18, 1970.

(Tennessee Code Annotated, Title 53, Chapter 34, Sections 3408 to 3422, 1967 Cumulative Supplement.)

Texas

The Clean Air Act of Texas was adopted in 1965 and amended in 1967. The act created the Texas Air Control Board and empowered the Board to develop a plan for proper control of the air resources of Texas, to adopt and promulgate rules and regulations, and to make investigations, hold hearings, and enter orders as necessary to effectuate the purposes of the act.

Regulations, ordinances, or resolutions of other state or local agencies now or hereafter in effect are not superseded by the act, provided they are consistent with the rules and regulations of the Board.

Regulations have been adopted by the state covering smoke and suspended particulate matter, outdoor burning, sulfur compounds, and motor vehicles.

(Vernon's Civil Statutes of the State of Texas Annotated, Title 71, Chapter Four A, Article 4477-5, Sections 1-19, 1967 Cumulative Pocket Part.)

Utah

In 1967 the state legislature provided for the creation of The Air Conservation Council within the state Department of Health. The Council has the power and duty to promulgate, adopt, amend, and repeal rules and regulations, establish air quality standards, hold hearings, cause the institution of legal proceedings, and grant variances. The act empowers the Executive Secretary of the Council to carry out the purposes of the act and to represent the state in interstate air pollution control compacts or agreements.

Any political subdivision is empowered to act alone or with other political subdivisions to enforce ordinances consistent with the act. Upon failure to comply with an order, the Council is authorized to initiate an action for injunctive relief.

(Chapter 47, Laws 1967.)

Vermont

A 1968 Vermont law designates the State Board of Health as the state air pollution control agency. The Board was given the power to prepare comprehensive abatement plans, hold hearings, adopt rules to implement the act, issue orders, establish ambient air quality standards, and consult with persons proposing to construct any facility that might be related to air pollution.

Municipalities within the state are permitted to establish and administer their own air pollution control programs with the approval of the Board.

(No. 310, Acts of 1967, approved March 22, 1968.)

Virginia

In 1966 the Air Pollution Control Act established a state Air Pollution Control Board. The Board is empowered to adopt rules and regulations, grant local variances therefrom, initiate and receive complaints, create local control districts, hold hearings, and represent the state in negotiations. Failure to comply with the regulations is punishable by fine.

Regulations adopted by the Board set limits on smoke, open burning, dust, and fumes.

(Code of Virginia, 1950, Annotated, Title 10, Chapter 1.2, Sections 1.2 and 10-17.10 to .30, 1966 Supplement.)

Washington

In 1967, by the Washington Clean Air Act, the State Air Pollution Control Board was given the same powers and duties as those conferred upon the governing body of any city, town, county, or the board of any activated authority or activated regional authority. In addition, the Board may adopt ambient air quality controls, adopt requirements for the control or prohibition of emissions of air contaminants to the outdoor atmosphere, cooperate with appropriate governmental officials with respect to air pollution controls or in formulating interstate compacts, conduct air quality studies, enforce requirements for control and emission prohibitions, and encourage local units of government to handle air pollution problems. The law provides for injunctions and fines and/or imprisonment.

Agencies formed under the Clean Air Act include the Puget Sound Air Pollution Control Agency (Snohomish, King, and Pierce Counties), the Northwest Air Pollution Authority (Skagit and Whatcom Counties), the Southwestern Air Pollution Control Authority (Clark, Cowlitz, Lewis, Skamania, and Wahkiakum Counties) the Thurston County Air Pollution Control Authority, and agencies in Spokane and Yakima Counties.

(Chapter 238, Laws 1967, amending Revised Code of Washington, Chapter 70.94.)

West Virginia

In 1961 West Virginia enacted a statewide air pollution control statute and established an Air Pollution Control Commission to administer the act. The Commission is authorized to develop ways to control air pollution, promulgate rules and regulations, conduct studies, hold hearings, enter orders requiring compliance with the statute and regulations, and appoint technical advisory councils. The Commission may enter orders requiring compliance with the statute and regulations. A violation of an order is punishable by penalty. In the absence of reasonable progress toward correction of an order, the Commission may seek an injunction.

In addition, the 1967 legislature ratified an interstate compact on air pollution between Ohio and West Virginia.

A statewide regulation to prevent and control air pollution from coal refuse disposal areas was adopted in 1965. Regulations to prevent and control air pollution from combustion of fuel in indirect heat exchangers within the Kanawha Valley air basin and to prevent and control air pollution by reason of the operation of mix asphalt plants were adopted in 1966. Other regulations on open burning and on coal preparation plants have been approved.

(Article 20, Chapter 60, West Virginia Code, as amended and reenacted by SB 200 and SB 270, approved March 17, 1967.)

Wisconsin

A 1967 law made the Department of Resource Development the statewide agency for the control of air and water pollution and solid wastes.

The Department has powers to prepare comprehensive abatement plans, conduct research, consult with persons planning to construct facilities, promulgate rules to implement the law, hold hearings, issue orders, and make inspections. An Air Pollution Control Advisory Council advises the Department. The law contains local option provisions.

(Chapter 83, Laws 1967.)

Wyoming

The 1967 Wyoming Air Quality Act provided authority to prevent, control, and abate air pollution in Wyoming. An Air Resources Council was created in the Department of Public Health and was empowered to devise, formulate, adopt, amend, and repeal rules and regulations, standards, and methods of procedure for preventing or reducing air pollution. The Division of Administration, Department of Public Health, was directed to enforce and administer the act and the rules, regulations, standards, and orders promulgated and issued thereunder. The act does not make provision for local control programs.

Ambient air quality standards for particulate emissions have been adopted.

(Chapter 186, Laws 1967.)

APPENDIX A

California

Excerpts from the Health and Safety Code of the State of California, as amended by the Pure Air Act of 1968

Division 1

Part 1

CHAPTER 2

Article 9. Air Sanitation

425. The State Department of Public Health shall submit to the State Air Resources Board recommendations for ambient air quality standards reflecting the relationship between the intensity and composition of air pollution and the health, illness, irritation to the senses, and the death of human beings.

Division 26. Mulford-Carrell Air Resources Act

Part 1. Air Resources Board

CHAPTER 1. GENERAL PROVISIONS

39000. This division may be cited as the Mulford-Carrell Air Resources Act.

Article 1. Definitions

39001. "Board" means the State Air Resources Board.

39002. "County district" means a county air pollution control district established under Chapter 2 (commencing with Section 24198 of Division 20).

39003. "County district board" means the board of directors of a county district.

39004. "Basin" means an area of the state designated by the board.

39005. "Regional district" means a regional air polution control district established pursuant to Part 2 (commencing with Section 39300) of this division.

39006. "Regional board" means the board of directors of a regional district.

39007. "Vehicular sources" means those sources of air pollution emitted from motor vehicles or vehicles, as defined in Section 415 and 670 of the Vehicle Code.

39008. "Nonvehicular sources" means all sources of air pollution except vehicular sources.

39008.5. "Ambient air quality standards" means specified concentrations and durations of pollutants which reflect the relationship between the intensity and composition of pollution to undesirable effects.

39009. "Emission standards" means specified limitations on the discharge of pollutants into the atmosphere.

39009.3. As used in this part and in Section 14808.1 of the Government Code, the low emission standard is an emission standard more stringent than the approval test standard. In establishing the low emission standard the board shall attempt to insure that no more than 50 percent of the new motor vehicles sold and registered in California that year would be able to comply with the low emission standard.

39009.5. "Local or regional authority" includes the governing body of any city, county, city and county, and of any air pollution control district which is functioning and exercising its powers.

Article 2. Declaration of Policy

39010. The Legislature finds and declares that the people of the State of California have a primary interest in the quality of the physical environment in which they live, and that this physical environment is being degraded by the waste and refuse of civilization polluting the atmosphere, thereby creating a situation which is detrimental to the health, safety, welfare, and sense of well-being of the people of California.

39011. It is necessary to provide a means for an intensive coordinated state, regional, and local effort to combat the problems of air pollution within the various air basins in the state by dividing the state into basins based upon similar meteorological and geographical conditions and with consideration for political boundary lines wherever practicable, and to provide for state authority to establish ambient air quality standards that could vary from basin to basin as well as statewide motor vehicle emission standards, and to provide for control of emissions from nonvehicular sources.

39012. Local and regional authorities have the primary responsibility for the control of air pollution except for the emissions from motor vehicles. These authorities may control emissions from nonvehicular sources. In addition these authorities are empowered to establish standards more restrictive than those set by the state board. The state authority shall undertake enforcement activities only after it has determined that the local or regional authorities have failed to meet their responsibilities pursuant to the provisions of this division. Such determination shall only be made after a public hearing has been held for that purpose.

39013. It is imperative to provide a single state agency for administration, research, establishment of standards, and the coordination of air conservation activities carried on within the state.

CHAPTER 2. ADMINISTRATION

39020. There is in state government the State Air Resources Board. The board shall consist of 14 members, 9 of whom shall be appointed by the Governor with the consent of the Senate. The Governor shall consider demonstrated interest and proven ability in the field of air pollution as well as the needs of the general public, industry, agriculture, and other related interests, in making appointments to the board. The Director of Public Health, Director of Motor Vehicles, Director of Agriculture, Commissioner of the California Highway Patrol, and Director of Conservation shall serve as members of the board. The Governor shall appoint the chairman from one of the nine appointees who shall serve as chairman at the pleasure of the Governor.

39021. Of the nine members originally appointed by the Governor, three shall be appointed to serve until July 1, 1969, three shall be appointed to serve until July 1, 1970, and three shall be appointed to serve until July 1, 1971. Thereafter, all members shall be appointed for a term of four years. All members shall hold office until the appointment of their successors. Any vacancies shall be immediately filled by the Governor for the unexpired portion of the term in which they occur. Members shall serve without compensation but each member shall be reimbursed for his necessary traveling and other expenses incurred in the performance of his duties under this division.

39022. The board shall appoint a 12-member technical advisory committee consisting of physicians, scientists, biologists, chemists, engineers, or meteorologists each of whom has had professional or technical experience in the field of air pollution. These committee members shall receive fifty dollars ($50) per day for each day they meet to fulfill the purposes of this act plus necessary traveling and other expenses incurred while performing their duties under this division.

39023. The board shall appoint an executive officer and may contract for services and may employ such technical and other personnel and acquire such facilities and may call upon the Department of Public Health as may be necessary for the performance of its powers and duties in carrying out the provisions of this division. The board may appoint such advisory groups and committees as it requires to effectuate the purpose of this division.

CHAPTER 3. POWERS AND DUTIES

39051. The board shall after holding public hearings:

(a) Divide the state into basins to fulfill the purposes of this division not later than January 1, 1969.

(b) Adopt standards of ambient air quality for each basin in consideration of the public health, safety and welfare, including but not limited to health, illness, irritation to the senses, aesthetic value, interference with visibility, and effects on the economy. These standards may vary from one basin to another. Standards relating to health effects shall be based upon the recommendations of the State Department of Public Health.

(c) Adopt rules and regulations in accordance with the provisions of the Administrative Procedure Act (commencing with Section 11370 of the Government Code) necessary for the proper execution of the powers and duties granted to, and imposed upon, the board by this division.

(d) Adopt emission standards of all other air pollution sources for application for each basin as found necessary as provided in Section 39054.

39052. The board shall:

(a) Conduct studies and evaluate the effects of air pollution upon human, plant, and animal life and the factors responsible for air pollution. The board may call upon the Department of Public Health, Department of Agriculture, the University of California, and such other state agencies it may deem necessary.

(b) Encourage a cooperative state effort in combating air pollution.

(c) Inventory sources of air pollution within the basins of the state and determine the kinds and quantity of air pollutants. The board shall use, to the fullest extent, the data of local agencies in fulfilling this purpose.

(d) Monitor air pollutants in cooperation with other agencies to fulfill the purpose of this division.

(e) Coordinate and collect research data on air pollution.

(f) Review rules and regulations of local or regional authorities filed with it pursuant to Sections 39314 and 39461 to assure that reasonable provision is made to control emissions from nonvehicular sources and to achieve the air quality standards established by the board.

(g) Adopt formal procedures, after consultation with the Department of Motor Vehicles, for making timely and decisive mutual agreements on vehicle air pollution matters with which both agencies are concerned, and submit a copy of these procedures to the Legislature by January 1, 1969.

(h) Adopt formal procedures, after consultation with the Department of Public Health, for the performance of services required by the board and for evaluating and resolving air pollution matters with which both agencies are concerned, and submit a copy of these procedures to the Legislature by January 1, 1969.

(i) Adopt formal procedures, after consultation with the Department of the California Highway Patrol, for making timely and decisive mutual agreements on vehicle air pollution matters with which both agencies are concerned, and submit a copy of these procedures to the Legislature by January 1, 1969.

(j) Publish annually a report of the results of the tests administered pursuant to subdivision (k) of this section, which shall include all of the following:

(1) The total number of motor vehicles tested.

(2) The total number of each engine and transmission combination tested.

(3) The average emissions of all motor vehicles tested.

(4) The average emissions of each engine and transmission combination tested.

(5) An analysis of the emissions of each engine and transmission combination tested.

(k) Adopt test procedures as soon as possible, but in no event later than 45 days after the effective date of the amendments to this section enacted by the Legislature at the 1968 Regular Session, specifying the manner in which new motor vehicles shall be approved based upon the emission standards contained in Article 2 (commencing with Section 39100) of Chapter 4 of this part. The board shall base its test procedures on driving patterns typical in the urban areas of California, and shall weight approval standards appropriately to reflect normal engine deposit accumulation.

The board shall administer the test for new motor vehicles in accordance with such procedures.

(l) Adopt regulations specifying the manner in which used motor vehicles shall be accredited based upon their emissions. These regulations are to be submitted to the Legislature by January 1, 1969.

(m) Adopt regulations specifying the manner in which motor vehicles on factory assembly lines are to be emission tested. Such tests shall take into consideration the recommendations of the Technical Advisory Panel to the Assembly Transportation and Commerce Committee as set forth in its report of April 14, 1968. Board regulations shall require manufacturers to submit copies of their test procedures and the test results to the board. These regulations are to be submitted to the Legislature by March 31, 1969.

(n) Adopt exhaust emission standards for hydrocarbons, carbon monoxide, and oxides of nitrogen for new diesel-powered vehicles, and diesel engines for vehicles first sold and registered in this state, no later than January 1, 1971.

(o) Adopt emission standards for motor vehicles which shall be applicable only to motor vehicles for which emission standards have not been specified in Article 2 (commencing with Section 39100) of Chapter 4 of this part.

(p) Adopt low emission standards for the purpose of carrying out Section 14808.1 of the Government Code and Section 6377 of the Revenue and Taxation Code for each model year motor vehicle beginning 1970.

39052.5. The board may adopt motor vehicle emission standards more stringent than those specified in Article 2 (commencing with Section 39100) of Chapter 4 of this part, which the board has found to be necessary and technologically feasible to carry out the purposes of this part.

39052.6. The board may adopt and implement motor vehicle emission standards for the control of other contaminants and sources of air pollution which are not included within Article 2 (commencing with Section 39100) of Chapter 4 of this part, which the board has found to be necessary and technologically feasible to carry out the purposes of this part.

39053. The board may provide assistance to local and regional agencies in effectuating all the provisions of this division.

39054. If the board finds after investigation and testing that its ambient air quality standards are not being complied with within a basin or that any local or regional authority has not taken reasonable action to control emissions from nonvehicular sources, it may request a report from such local or regional authority as to the action taken to control the sources responsible. If the board's investigation and testing reveals that its standards are not being complied with, or the local or regional standards are not being complied with or are inadequate, and that the report of the local or regional authority is unsatisfactory, the board may hold public hearings. If the board after holding public hearings, is still unsatisfied it may issue a statement of findings, and may direct the local or regional authority, to take further reasonable action. If any local or regional authority does not comply with the directive of the board within 30 days after the date of the directive, the board shall enforce the standards and the rules and regulations adopted by the board pursuant to this part within the area under the jurisdiction of such local or regional authority until such time as the directive is withdrawn by the board or the local or regional authority complies with the directive. The board may take any other appropriate legal action to carry out its responsibilities in such area. The board shall also have the authority, if such area is within any air pollution control district which is functioning and exercising its powers, to take any action which the district may take. If such area is not within an air pollution control district which is functioning and exercising its powers, the board shall also have the authority to take any action which Chapter 2 (commencing with Section 24198) of Division 20 authorizes a district which is functioning and exercising its powers under that chapter to take. Every person who violates any standard, rule or regulation adopted by the board pursuant to this part in any area in which such standards, rules, and regulations are being enforced by the board is guilty of a misdemeanor. Every day during any portion of which such violation occurs constitutes a separate offense.

39055. The board shall be empowered to hold hearings for the purpose of fulfilling the provisions of this division.

39056. Nothing shall prevent individual counties within a basin from establishing their own county boards while the remaining counties in the same basin establish a regional board.

39057. Notwithstanding the provisions of this division, any local or regional authority may establish additional, more strict standards than those set forth by the state board for all sources of air pollution other than motor vehicles.

39058. The standards, rules, and regulations adopted by a local or regional authority shall be filed with the state board. Such standards, rules, and regulations may be more restrictive than those adopted by the board.

39059. No county, except a county which on the operative date of this section is within an air pollution control district which is functioning and exercising its powers, shall be required to be represented on a regional board, or to have its own board, unless and until the board of supervisors, as authorized by Section 24205, adopt a resolution declaring that there is need for an air pollution control district to function or, as authorized by Part 2 (commencing with Section 39300) of this division, a resolution is adopted by the board of supervisors of the county and by the board of supervisors of one or more other counties declaring that there is a need for a regional district to function, in a common region including all or any portion of such counties and certified copies of the resolution are filed with the State Air Resources Board as provided in Section 39354.

39060. The board is designated as the state air pollution control agency for the purpose of cooperating with the federal government.

39061. The board shall administer any statewide program of financial assistance for air pollution control which may be delegated to it by law and may accept funds from the United States or other source to that end. The board may conduct such a program independently, or by contract, or in cooperation with any federal or state agency, including any political subdivision of the state, or any person or public or private organization.

39062. The board shall submit a report to the Governor and the Legislature not later than 10 calendar days following the commencement of each general session of the Legislature consisting of a summary of the board's activities during the previous year and the board's recommendations concerning such legislation and other action as is necessary for the implementation, financing, and enforcement of this division.

39063. All facilities, including but not limited to funds, records, equipment, and personnel of the State Vehicular Pollution Laboratory of the State Department of Public Health in Los Angeles over which the department has control are hereby transferred to the State Air Resources Board.

39064. The Motor Vehicle Pollution Control Board is abolished. All facilities, including but not limited to funds, records, equipment, and personnel of the Motor Vehicle Pollution Control Board are hereby transferred to the State Air Resources Board.

39065. All present standards and rules and regulations for the purposes of air pollution control established by the State Department of Public Health and the Motor Vehicle Pollution Control Board shall remain in effect until the State Air Resources Board incorporates them into its rules and regulations or standards or adopts rules and regulations or standards.

39066. This division shall not be deemed to affect any rule or regulation of any county or regional district which is in effect on the effective date of this division until the State Air Resources Board has reviewed the rules and regulations of the district.

CHAPTER 4. MOTOR VEHICLE POLLUTION CONTROL

Article 1. Application and Definitions

39080. This chapter may be cited as the "Pure Air Act of 1968."

39081. The Legislature finds and declares:

(a) That the emission of pollutants from motor vehicles is the primary cause of air pollution in many portions of the state.

(b) That the control and elimination of such pollutants is of prime importance for the protection and preservation of the public health and well-being, and for the prevention of irritation to the senses, interference with visibility, and damage to vegetation and property.

(c) That the state has a responsibility to establish uniform procedures for compliance with standards which control or eliminate such pollutants.

(d) That the California goal for pure air quality is the achievement of an atmosphere with no significant detectable adverse effect from motor vehicle air pollution on health, welfare and the quality of life and property by 1975.

(e) That vehicle emission standards applied to new motor vehicles and to used motor vehicles equipped with emission control devices are standards with which all such vehicles shall comply subject to the approval, accreditation, and certification provisions of this part.

39082. The provisions of this chapter shall not apply to any racing vehicle, as defined in Section 39090.5.

39083. The provisions of this chapter shall not apply to any limited production motor vehicle, as defined in Section 39090.

39083.5. The provisions of this chapter shall not apply to any motorcycle as defined in Section 39084.

39084. As used in this chapter the following terms shall be construed as defined in the Vehicle Code:

(a) Commercial vehicle
(b) Implement of husbandry
(c) Motor vehicle
(d) Motorcycle
(e) Used vehicle
(f) Passenger vehicle
(g) New vehicle
(h) Truck
(i) Truck tractor
(j) Bus

39085. As used in this chapter, "approval" means the findings of the board that the device for new vehicles has satisfied the tests and procedures established by the board to determine whether the various makes and models of new motor vehicles for each model year may be sold and registered in this state. Approval shall be determined on the basis of motor vehicle emissions and such other related factors as the board may in regulations indicate.

39086. As used in this chapter, "crankcase emissions" means substances emitted directly to the atmosphere from any opening leading to the crankcase of a motor vehicle engine. Crankcase gases which are conducted to the engine intake or exhaust systems are not included in the definition of crankcase emissions, but are defined as exhaust emissions.

39087. As used in this chapter, "exhaust emissions" means substances emitted to the atmosphere from any opening downstream from the exhaust port of a motor vehicle engine.

39088. As used in this chapter, "fuel evaporative loss emissions" means vaporized fuel emitted into the atmosphere from the fuel system of a motor vehicle.

39089. As used in this chapter, "fuel system" means the combination of fuel tank, fuel lines and carburetor, or fuel injector, and includes all vents and fuel evaporative emission control systems or devices.

39090. As used in this chapter, "limited production vehicle" means a make of motor vehicle manufactured in quantities of less than 2,000 units for any given model year.

39090.5. As used in this chapter, "racing vehicle" means a competition vehicle not used on public roads or highways.

39091. As used in this chapter, "model year" means the time of actual manufacture either (1) within the annual production period of such vehicles as designated by the calendar year in which such period ends, or (2) if the manufacturer does not so designate the annual production period of such vehicles manufactured by him, within the 12-month period beginning November 1 of the preceding year. In the case of any vehicle manufactured in two or more stages, the time of manufacture shall be the date of completion of the chassis.

39092. As used in this chapter, "accreditation" means a finding by the board, pursuant to the procedures established in Article 5 (commencing with Section 39175) of this chapter, that a used motor vehicle emission control device has satisfied the tests and procedures established by the board pursuant to Sections 39107 and 39108.

39093. As used in this chapter, "motor vehicle pollution control device" means equipment designed for installation on a motor vehicle for the purpose of reducing the pollutants emitted from the vehicle, or a system or engine modification on a motor vehicle which causes a reduction of pollutants emitted from the vehicle.

39094. As used in this chapter, "certified device" means a motor vehicle pollution control device required to be installed on various motor vehicles under regulations adopted by the former Motor Vehicle Pollution Control Board prior to November 8, 1967, or under regulations adopted by the board prior to the effective date of the applicable standards provided in this part.

39095. As used in this chapter other than in Section 39094, "Motor Vehicle Pollution Control Board" means, and is applicable to, the board.

39096. As used in this chapter, the terms hydrocarbons, carbon monoxide, and oxides of nitrogen, shall be construed as defined in the regulations of the board, such definitions to be developed in accordance with the purpose of this chapter.

Article 2. Motor Vehicle Emission Standards

39100. Approval of new motor vehicles for sale and registration and accreditation of devices for used motor vehicles shall be contingent upon compliance with the standards established in this part or pursuant thereto, under the test procedures established by the board pursuant to Section 39052. Motor vehicles which do not so comply with the applicable standards shall not be sold and registered in California.

39100.1. Every manufacturer of motor vehicles sold in the State of California during the calendar year 1968 shall file with the board, not later than 60 days after the effective date of this section, a report describing such manufacturer's research and development activities, including test data, during the preceding 12 months relating to the control of oxides of nitrogen emitted from its vehicles. Where proprietary or competitive requirements necessitate, such reports shall refer to vehicles, technical innovations, and devices by code name or number. Additional progress reports shall be filed with the board by such manufacturers at three-month intervals from 60 days after the effective date of this section until July 1, 1970. Failure to submit such reports shall be considered as constituting failure of compliance under Section 39154.

39100.5. The standards in this article have been found to be technologically feasible and capable of implementation with reasonable economic cost by a technical advisory panel of nine California engineers, scientists, and air pollution experts.

39101. The exhaust emissions from a new 1970 model year gasoline-powered motor vehicle under 6,001 pounds, manufacturer's maximum gross vehicle weight rating having an engine displacement of 50 cubic inches or greater, subject to registration and first sold and registered in this state, shall not exceed:

(a) 2.2 grams per mile hydrocarbons.

(b) 23 grams per mile carbon monoxide.

39101.5. The exhaust emissions from a new 1971 model year gaso-line-powered motor vehicle under 6,001 pounds, manufacturer's maxi-mum gross vehicle weight rating having an engine displacement of 50 cubic inches or greater, subject to registration and first sold and registered in this state, shall not exceed:

(a) 2.2 grams per mile hydrocarbons.

(b) 23 grams per mile carbon monoxide.

(c) 4.0 grams per mile oxides of nitrogen.

39102. The exhaust emissions from a new 1972 or later model year gasoline-powered motor vehicle under 6,001 pounds, manufacturer's maximum gross vehicle weight rating having an engine displacement of 50 cubic inches or greater, subject to registration and first sold and registered in this state, shall not exceed:

(a) 1.5 grams per mile hydrocarbons.

(b) 23 grams per mile carbon monoxide.

(c) 3.0 grams per mile oxides of nitrogen.

39102.5. Notwithstanding the provisions of subdivision (c) of Sec-tion 39102, the oxides of nitrogen exhaust emissions from a new 1974 or later model year gasoline-powered motor vehicles under 6,001 pounds, manufacturer's maximum gross vehicle weight rating having an engine displacement of 50 cubic inches or greater, subject to registration and first sold and registered in this state, shall not exceed 1.3 grams per mile oxides of nitrogen.

39014. The exhaust emissions from a new 1970 or 1971 model year gasoline-powered truck, truck tractor or bus, except those which are diesel-powered, over 6,001 pounds, manufacturer's maximum gross vehicle weight rating, subject to registration and first sold and registered in this state, shall not exceed:

(a) 275 parts per million hydrocarbons.

(b) 1.5 percent carbon monoxide.

39105. The exhaust emissions from a new 1972 or later model year gasoline-powered truck, truck tractor or bus, except those which are die-sel-powered, over 6,001 pounds, manufacturer's maximum gross vehicle weight rating, subject to registration and first sold and registered in this state, shall not exceed:

(a) 180 parts per million hydrocarbons.

(b) 1.0 percent carbon monoxide.

39106. Fuel evaporative losses from the fuel system in a 1970 or later model year gasoline-powered motor vehicle having an engine dis-placement of 50 cubic inches or greater, under 6,001 pounds, manufac-turer's maximum gross vehicle weight rating, subject to registration and first sold and registered in this state, shall not exceed six grams hydrocar-bons per test.

39107. In order for an exhaust emission device to be accredited by the board pursuant to Article 5 (commencing with Section 39175) of this chapter it shall not allow emissions exceeding any of the following:

(a) 275 parts per million hydrocarbons.

(b) 1.5 percent carbon monoxide.

39108. In order for an evaporative loss device to be accredited by the board pursuant to Article 5 (commencing with Section 39175) of this chapter, it shall not allow fuel system evaporative loss greater than six grams hydrocarbons per test.

39109. Exhaust emission standards for hydrocarbons, carbon monoxide and oxides of nitrogen for new diesel-powered vehicles first sold and registered in this state as established by the board pursuant to subdivision (n) of Section 39052, shall apply to all such vehicles at such time as the board determines it is technologically feasible, but no later than January 1, 1973.

Article 3. Previously Certified Devices

39125. All motor vehicles previously required to have certified pollution control devices pursuant to the provisions of Chapter 1545, Statutes of 1967, shall be required to continue to have such devices, unless otherwise specifically exempted by this chapter.

39126. The board may exempt classifications of motor vehicles subject to this article for which certified devices are not available and motor vehicles whose emissions are found by appropriate tests to meet state standards without additional equipment, and motor-driven cycles, implements of husbandry, and vehicles which qualify for special license plates under Section 5004 of the Vehicle Code.

39127. The board may revoke, suspend, or restrict a certificate of a previously certified device or an exemption previously granted upon a determination by the board that the device no longer operates within the standards set by the board or no longer should be exempted. Provided that once any motor vehicle is equipped with a certified device it shall not thereafter be deemed in violation of this chapter or of Section 27156 of the Vehicle Code, because the certification of such device is subsequently revoked, suspended or restricted, and replacement parts for such device may continue to be supplied and used for such vehicle, unless such revocation, suspension or restriction is based upon a finding that the certified device has been found to be unsafe in actual use or is otherwise mechanically defective, in which event such devices shall be brought into compliance with this chapter within 30 days after such finding.

39128. Proceedings under this chapter with respect to the granting of exemptions, or for the revocation, suspension or restriction of certificates previously issued, or exemptions previously granted, by the board, shall be conducted in accordance with the provisions of Chapter 5 (commencing with Section 11500), Part 1, Division 3, Title 2 of the Government Code, and the board shall have all the powers granted therein.

39129. The following classifications of motor vehicles are subject to the provisions of this article:

(a) Every 1966 or later year model motor vehicle subject to registration in this state shall be equipped with a certified device or devices to control emission of pollutants from the crankcase and exhaust.

(b) Every motor vehicle of 1963 or later year model, subject to registration in this state shall be equipped with a certified device to control the emission of pollutants from the crankcase.

(c) Every motor vehicle of 1955 through 1962 year model subject to registration in this state upon transfer of ownership and registration to an owner whose residence is in a county or portion of a county within an air pollution control district which may function and exercise its powers shall be equipped with a certified device to control the emission of pollutants from the crankcase.

(d) Every motor vehicle of 1955 through 1965 year model subject to registration in this state upon transfer of ownership and registration to an owner whose residence is in a county or portion of a county within an air pollution control district which may function and exercise its powers, shall be equipped with a certified device to control the emission of pollutants from the exhaust.

(e) The provisions of subdivisions (a), (b), (c), and (d) of this section shall not be applicable to any of the following vehicles:

(1) Any motor vehicle or class of motor vehicles exempted by the board.

(2) Any motor-driven cycle, implement of husbandry or vehicle which qualifies for special plates under Section 5004 of the Vehicle Code.

(f) The provisions of subdivisions (c) and (d) shall not be applicable in any district activated after July 1, 1959, so as to be able to perform its functions unless the board of supervisors of each county in which the district is situated adopts a resolution based upon its finding that subdivisions (c) and (d) are necessary to the preservation of air quality within that district; nor shall the provisions of subdivisions (c) and (d) be applicable in any county situated within a multicounty district formed prior to July 1, 1959, which county is adjacent to a district activated prior to January 1, 1960, unless the board of supervisors in such county adopts a resolution based upon its finding that subdivisions (c) and (d) are necessary to the preservation of air quality within that county.

(g) Every 1968 year model passenger vehicle, except motorcycles, subject to registration and first sold and registered in this state shall be equipped with a certified device or devices to control emission of pollutants from the crankcases and exhaust. Notwithstanding any other provision of this section or of Article 5 (commencing with Section 39175) of this chapter, the board may only grant an exemption for not to exceed 1 percent of a manufacturer's passenger vehicle sales in California in the preceding model year.

(h) Every 1967 year model commercial motor vehicle under 6,001 pounds manufacturer's maximum gross vehicle weight rating subject to registration and first sold and registered in this state shall be equipped with a certified device or devices to control emission of pollutants from the crankcase and exhaust.

(i) The provisions of subdivisions (c) and (d) of this section shall not be applicable to motor vehicles registered to an owner whose residence is in an area, designated pursuant to this subdivision, of any county having an area in excess of 7,000 square miles in which an air pollution control district consisting of a single county may function and exercise its powers and within 60 days after the effective date of this section the board of supervisors of such county has classified the county into two areas because of substantial geographic and climatic differences between the two areas, and within 60 days after the effective date of this section the board of supervisors of the county has found that within one of such areas, designated by the board, the equipment of motor vehicles with devices to control the emission of pollutants is unnecessary for the preservation of air quality within that area.

(j) Notwithstanding any provision of subdivision (f), if after the effective date of this section subdivisions (c) and (d) are made applicable to a district or county in which subdivisions (c) and (d) are inapplicable under subdivision (f) on such effective date, subdivisions (c) and (d) shall not be applicable to any other district or county unless its governing board adopts a resolution based upon its finding that subdivisions (c) and (d) are necessary to the preservation of air quality in such other district or county, as the case may be.

39130. No person shall sell, display, advertise, or represent as a certified device any device which, in fact, is not a certified device. No person shall install or sell for installation upon any motor vehicle, any motor vehicle pollution control device which has not been certified by the board.

39131. Any manufacturer of a device required by this article shall, as a condition of certification of such device by the board, agree that so long as only one such device is certified by the board such manufacturer shall either: (1) agree to enter into such cross-licensing or other agreements as the board determines are necessary to insure adequate competition among manufacturers of such devices to protect the public interest; or (2) agree as a condition to such certification that if only one such device from one manufacturer is made available for sale to the public, the board shall, taking into consideration the cost of manufacturing the device and the manufacturer's suggested retail price, and in order to protect the public interest, determine the fair and reasonable retail price of such device and may require, as a condition to continued certification of such device, that the retail price of such device, including installation, not exceed such price as determined by the board. In either event the retail price so determined by the board for a device required by subdivision (d) of Section 39129 or Section 39176 shall not be in excess of sixty-five dollars ($65) per vehicle.

Article 4. New Motor Vehicle Approval

39150. The board shall have the powers and authority necessary to carry out the duties imposed on it by this article including, but not limited to, the following:

(a) To adopt rules and regulations in accordance with the provisions of the Administrative Procedure Act (commencing with Section 11370) of the Government Code, necessary for proper execution of the powers and duties granted to, and imposed upon, the board by this article.

(b) To employ such technical and other personnel as may be necessary for the performance of its powers and duties.

39151. No new motor vehicle required pursuant to this part to meet the emission standards in Article 2 (commencing with Section 39100) of this chapter or the standards set pursuant to Sections 39052.5 or 39052.6

shall be sold and registered in this state unless the engine and transmission combination used in that vehicle has been approved by the board.

Vehicle manufacturers shall test engine and transmission combinations in vehicles which are representative of the types of vehicles in which that engine and transmission combination is used.

39154. No new motor vehicle required pursuant to this part to meet the emission standards in Article 2 (commencing with Section 39100) of this chapter shall be sold and registered in this state if the vehicle manufacturer has in the previous year for which the board approved his vehicles failed to comply with the standards established in this part or with such regulations as the board may establish, unless the manufacturer thereof complies with such other conditions as the board may by regulation indicate.

The procedures for determining, and the facts constituting, compliance and failure of compliance shall be established by the board pursuant to subdivision (c) of Section 39051.

Article 5. Used Motor Vehicle Device Accreditation

39175. The board shall have the powers and authority necessary to carry out the duties imposed on it by this article including, but not limited to, the following:

(a) To adopt rules and regulations in accordance with the provisions of the Administrative Procedure Act (commencing with Section 11370) of the Government Code, necessary for proper execution of the powers and duties granted to, and imposed upon the board by this article.

(b) To employ such technical and other personnel as may be necessary for the performance of its powers and duties.

(c) To determine and publish by January 1, 1969, tests and procedures for the accreditation of used car exhaust emission control and fuel system evaporative loss control devices.

(d) To accredit motor vehicle pollution control devices following tests by the board or by a board-designated laboratory in which the board finds that the device operates within the standards set in Article 2 (commencing with Section 39100) of this chapter or that the device effectively controls harmful pollutants not specifically mentioned in Article 2 (commencing with Section 39100) of this chapter, or that the device effectively controls emissions from a part of the vehicle not specifically mentioned in Article 2 (commencing with Section 39100) of this chapter. Any device accredited shall be technologically feasible.

39176. Whenever an exhaust emission control device is accredited pursuant to the provisions of this article and is available for installation as determined by the board, every 1955 through 1965 year model vehicle shall be equipped with an accredited device to control the emission of pollutants from the exhaust in accordance with the requirements, exemptions and schedule of installation provided in Article 3 (commencing with Section 39125) of this chapter.

39177. The board may exempt classifications of motor vehicles for which accredited devices are not available, and motor vehicles whose emissions are found by appropriate tests to meet state standards without additional equipment, and motor-driven cycles, implements of husbandry, and vehicles which qualify for special license plates under Section 5004 of the Vehicle Code.

39178. The board may revoke, suspend or restrict an accreditation of a previously accredited device or an exemption previously granted upon a determination by the board that the device no longer operates within the standards set by the board or no longer should be exempted. Provided that once any motor vehicle is equipped with an accredited device it shall not thereafter be deemed in violation of this chapter or Section 27156 of the Vehicle Code because the accreditation of such device is subsequently revoked, suspended or restricted, and replacement parts for such device may continue to be supplied and used for such vehicle, unless such revocation, suspension or restriction is based upon a finding that the accredited device has been found to be defective, in which event such devices must be brought into compliance with this chapter within 30 days after such finding.

39179. Proceedings under this article with respect to the denial of applications for accreditation, the granting of exemptions, or for the revocation, suspension, or restriction of accreditation previously granted by the board shall be conducted in accordance with the provisions of Chapter 5 (commencing with Section 11500), Part 1, Division 3, Title 2 of the Government Code, and the board shall have all the powers granted therein.

39180. In establishing tests and procedures the board shall adopt standards including, but not limited to, the following:

(a) An accredited exhaust emission control device shall not cost more than sixty-five dollars ($65), including the cost of installation.

(b) An accredited exhaust emission control device shall not require maintenance more than once each 12,000 miles, and such maintenance shall not cost more than fifteen dollars ($15), including the cost of parts and labor.

(c) An accredited exhaust control device shall equal or exceed the performance criteria established by the board for devices for new motor vehicles or, in the alternative, have an expected useful life of at least 50,000 miles of operation.

(d) Standards for an accredited fuel system evaporative loss control device shall take into consideration the cost of the device and its installation, its durability, the ease and facility of determining whether the device, when installed on a motor vehicle is properly functioning, and any other factors which, in the opinion of the board, render such a device suitable or unsuitable for the control of motor vehicle air pollution or for the health, safety, and welfare of the public.

(e) An accredited fuel system evaporative loss control device shall equal or exceed the performance criteria established by the board for such new devices required on new motor vehicles, or in the alternative, must have an expected useful life of at least 50,000 miles of operation.

39180.1. Whenever the board accredits a fuel system evaporative loss control device for which standards have been set by this chapter, it shall submit a report of its findings and its recommendations for installation on used vehicles to the Legislature within 10 days, if it is then in session, or if not in session not later than January 15, of the next general session. Such report shall contain a report on the cost of such device, including the cost of installation and a review of its potential performance, including required maintenance and the cost of parts and labor.

39180.2. No accredited fuel system evaporative loss control device for installation on used motor vehicles, nor any other accredited device not mentioned in Section 39129 shall be required to be installed on any used motor vehicles until approved by statute enacted by the Legislature.

39181. The board may issue permits for the testing of experimental motor pollution control devices installed in used motor vehicles, or for the testing of experimental or prototype motor vehicles which appear to have very low emission characteristics.

39182. Any manufacturer of a device required by this article shall, as a condition of accreditation of such device by the board, agree that so long as only one such device is accredited by the board such manufacturer shall either: (1) agree to enter into such cross-licensing or other agreements as the board determines are necessary to insure adequate competition among manufacturers of such devices to protect the public interest; or (2) agree as a condition to such accreditation that if only one such device from one manufacturer is made available for sale to the public, the board shall, taking into consideration the cost of manufacturing the device and the manufacturer's suggested retail price, and in order to protect the public interest, determine the fair and reasonable retail price of such device and may require as a condition to continued accreditation of such device, that the retail price of such device, including installation, not exceed such price as determined by the board. In either event the retail price so determined by the board for a device required by Section 39176 shall not exceed sixty-five dollars ($65) per vehicle.

39183. Whenever the board accredits a device for the control of emissions of pollutants from a particular source of emissions from motor vehicles for which standards have been set by this chapter and the board, it shall so notify the Department of Motor Vehicles.

39184. No person shall sell, display, advertise, or represent as an accredited device any device which, in fact, is not an accredited device. No person shall install or sell for installation upon any used motor vehicle any motor vehicle pollution control device which has not been accredited by the board.

Article 6. Variances

39190. The Governor with the advice and consent of the Senate shall appoint a hearing board to consist of three members, none of whom is employed by the board or the state. Two members shall be registered professional engineers knowledgeable in motor vehicle emission control. One member shall have been admitted to practice law in this state.

39191. The Governor shall appoint one member of the hearing board for a term of one year, one for a term of two years, and one for a term of three years. Thereafter the terms of members of the hearing board shall be three years.

39192. The hearing board at the request of any person may hold a hearing to determine under what conditions and to what extent a variance from the emission standards for new or used cars established by Article 2 (commencing with Section 39100) of this chapter or by rules, regulations, or orders of the board is necessary and will be permitted. All such hearings shall be open to the public and shall be held at a place which the board determines to be convenient to the public in the area most affected by the motor vehicle air pollution problem.

39193. The board may provide, by regulation, a schedule of fees which will yield a sum not exceeding the estimated cost of the administration of this article, for the filing of applications for variances or to revoke or modify variances. All applicants shall pay the fees required by such regulations.

39194. The hearing board shall serve a notice of the time and place of a hearing to grant a variance upon the chairman and the executive officer of the board and upon the applicant, if any, not less than 10 days prior to such hearing.

39195. If the hearing board finds that because of conditions beyond control, compliance with the standards in Article 2 (commencing with Section 39100) of this chapter or with any rule, regulation, or order of the board will result in an arbitrary and unreasonable taking of property or in a serious and demonstrable economic hardship without a sufficient corresponding benefit or advantage to the people in the reduction of air pollution, it shall prescribe other and different standards not more onerous applicable to named classes of industries or persons. Tests and procedures for determining compliance with the standards established by the hearing board shall be the same as those tests and procedures established by the State Air Resources Board.

In establishing other and different standards the hearing board shall not prescribe standards less onerous than any applicable federal standards. Any federal standard enacted or implemented during the period for which a variance granting a less onerous standard is running shall immediately supersede the standard established by the hearing board.

39196. Notwithstanding the provisions of Section 39195, the hearing board shall grant variances to manufacturers of new motor vehicles only on a showing that the vehicle manufacturer is making all reasonable efforts to comply with the standards as soon as possible.

39196.5. The hearing board may revoke or modify by written order, after a public hearing held upon not less than 10 days' notice, any order permitting a variance.

39197. The hearing board shall serve notice of the time and place of a hearing to revoke or modify any order permitting a variance not less than 10 days prior to such hearing upon the director and the executive officer of the board, upon all persons who will be subjected to greater restrictions if such order is revoked or modified as proposed and upon all other persons interested or likely to be affected who have filed with the hearing board or board a written request for such notification.

39197.5. The hearing board shall serve a notice of the time and place of a hearing to grant a variance or to revoke or modify an order permitting a variance either by personal service or by first-class mail, postage prepaid. If either the identity or address of any person entitled to notice is unknown, the hearing board shall serve such person by publication of notice once in a newspaper of general circulation published within the State of California.

39198. The hearing board in making any order permitting a variance may specify the time during which such order will be effective, in no event to exceed one year.

39199. The hearing board in administering the provisions of this article may conduct investigations and hearings pursuant to Article 2 (commencing with Section 11180), Chapter 2, Part 1, Division 3, Title 2 of the Government Code.

39200. After each hearing for a variance under proceedings held pursuant to this article, the hearing board shall make written findings of fact based upon the evidence and shall render a written decision. Such findings and written decision shall contain a detailed description of all testing data and testing procedures used in connection with the evidence submitted to the hearing board. Each written decision, accompanied by the findings, shall be transmitted to the Legislature forthwith. Nothing in this section shall require or authorize the disclosure of any trade secret privileged under Section 1060 of the Evidence Code, or of any information not a part of the public record the disclosure of which is prohibited by Section 11183 of the Government Code.

39201. The hearing board created by this article shall not exercise or undertake any duty, power, responsibility or jurisdiction vested in the hearing board by this article unless, and until, the State Air Resources Board determines that the Secretary of Health, Education and Welfare will not waive application to California of Section 208 of the National Emission Standards Act. In the event of such a determination by the State Air Resources Board then and then only shall Sections 39192 to 39200, inclusive, of this article become operative.

Sec. 9. Section 14808.1 is added to the Government Code, to read:

14808.1. In establishing bid specifications for the purchase of motor vehicles and in determining the lowest responsible bidder, consideration shall be given by the state to the low emission test results of such vehicles as determined by the State Air Resources Board pursuant to Section 39052 of the Health and Safety Code. The state shall purchase low emission test vehicles except for the following vehicles:

(a) Vehicles used by the Department of the California Highway Patrol as patrol cars.

(b) Vehicles which are used in other special ways so as to render the low emission requirements impractical.

Sec. 10. Section 2814 of the Vehicle Code is amended to read:

2814. Every driver of a passenger vehicle shall stop and submit the vehicle to an inspection of the mechanical condition and equipment of the vehicle at any location where members of the California Highway Patrol are conducting tests and inspections of passenger vehicles and when signs are displayed requiring such stop.

The Commissioner of the California Highway Patrol may make and enforce regulations with respect to the issuance of stickers or other devices to be displayed upon passenger vehicles as evidence that the vehicles have been inspected and have been found to be in safe mechanical condition and equipped as required by this code and equipped with certified motor vehicle pollution control devices as required by Chapter 4 (commencing with Section 39080) of Part 1 of Division 26 of the Health and Safety Code which are correctly installed and in operating condition. Any sticker so issued shall be placed on the windshield within a five-inch square in the extreme lower left corner thereof with respect to the driver's position.

If, upon such an inspection of a passenger vehicle, it is found to be in unsafe mechanical condition or not equipped as required by this code and the provisions of Chapter 4 (commencing with Section 39080) of Part 1 of Division 26 of the Health and Safety Code, the provisions of Article 2 (commencing with Section 40150) of Chapter 1 of Division 17 of this code shall apply.

Sec. 11. Section 4000 of the Vehicle Code is amended to read:

4000. (a) No person shall drive, move, or leave standing any motor vehicle, trailer, semitrailer, pole or pipe dolly, logging dolly, or auxiliary dolly upon a highway unless it is registered and the appropriate fees have been paid under this code.

No person shall drive, move, or leave standing any motor vehicle upon a highway which has been registered in violation of Chapter 4 (commencing with Section 39080) of Part 1 of Division 26 of the Health and Safety Code.

(b) The provisions of this section shall not apply, following payment of fees due for registration, during such time that registration and transfer is being withheld by the Department of Motor Vehicles pending the investigation of any use tax due under the provisions of the Revenue and Taxation Code.

(c) When a vehicle is towed by a tow car on order of a sheriff, marshal, or other official acting pursuant to a court order or on order of a peace officer acting pursuant to the provisions of Chapter 10 (commencing with Section 22650) of Division 11, the provisions of subdivision (a) of this section shall not apply.

Sec. 12. Section 4000.1 of the Vehicle Code is amended to read:

4000.1. (a) On and after December 1, 1965, the department shall require upon transfer of ownership and registration of any motor vehicle subject to Chapter 4 (commencing with Section 39080) of Part 1 of Division 26 of the Health and Safety Code, a valid certificate of compliance from a licensed motor vehicle pollution control device installation and inspection station indicating that such vehicle is properly equipped with a certified device or devices which are in proper operating condition and which are in compliance with the provisions of Chapter 4 (commencing with Section 39080) of Part 1 of Division 26 of the Health and Safety Code.

(b) The State Air Resources Board established under Chapter 4 (commencing with Section 39080) of Part 1 of Division 26 of the Health and Safety Code may exempt designated classifications of motor vehicles from the provisions of subdivision (a) as they deem necessary, and shall notify the department of such action; provided, however, that no exemption shall be granted to those vehicles subject to the provisions of subdivision (g) of Section 39129 of the Health and Safety Code, except as provided therein.

Sec. 13. Section 4750 of the Vehicle Code is amended to read:

4750. The department shall refuse registration or renewal or transfer of registration upon any of the following grounds:

(a) That the application contains any false or fraudulent statement.

(b) That the required fee has not been paid.

(c) That the registration or renewal or transfer of registration is prohibited by the requirements of Chapter 4 (commencing with Section 39080) of Part 1 of Division 26 of the Health and Safety Code.

Sec. 14. Section 24007 of the Vehicle Code is amended to read:

24007. (a) No dealer or person holding a retail seller's permit shall sell a new or used motor vehicle which is not in compliance with the provisions of this code and department regulations adopted pursuant to this code unless the vehicle is sold to another dealer or for the purpose of being wrecked or dismantled or is sold exclusively for off-highway use.

(b) No dealer shall sell a new or used motor vehicle subject to the provisions of Chapter 4 (commencing with Section 39080) of Part 1 of Division 26 of the Health and Safety Code which is not in compliance with the provisions of Chapter 4 (commencing with Section 39080) of Part 1 of Division 26 of the Health and Safety Code and the rules and regulations of the State Air Resources Board, unless the vehicle is sold to another dealer or for the purpose of being wrecked or dismantled. The dealer shall, with each application for transfer of registration of every 1955 or later year model motor vehicle subject to Chapter 4 (commencing with Section 39080) of Part 1 of Division 26 of the Health and Safety Code, transmit to the Department of Motor Vehicles a valid certificate of compliance from a licensed motor vehicle pollution control device installation and inspection station indicating that such vehicle is properly equipped with a certified device or devices which are in proper operating condition and which are in compliance with the provisions of Chapter 4 (commencing with Section 39080) of Part 1 of Division 26 of the Health and Safety Code.

Sec. 15. Section 27153.5 is added to the Vehicle Code, to read:

27153.5. (a) No motor vehicle first sold or registered as a new motor vehicle on or after January 1, 1971, shall discharge into the atmosphere at elevation of less than 3,000 feet any air contaminant for a period of more than 10 seconds which is:

(1) As dark or darker in shade as that designated as No. 1 on the Ringelmann Chart, as published by the United States Bureau of Mines, or

(2) Of such opacity as to obscure an observer's view to a degree equal to or greater than does smoke described in paragraph (1) of this subdivision.

(b) No motor vehicle first sold or registered prior to January 1, 1971, shall discharge into the atmosphere at elevation of less than 3,000 feet any air contaminant for a period of more than 10 seconds which is:

(1) As dark or darker in shade than that designated as No. 2 on the Ringelmann Chart, as published by the United States Bureau of Mines, or

(2) Of such opacity as to obscure an observer's view to a degree equal to or greater than does smoke described in paragraph (1) of this subdivision.

Sec. 16. Section 27156 of the Vehicle Code is amended to read:

27156. No person shall operate or leave standing upon any highway any motor vehicle which is required to be equipped with a certified motor vehicle pollution control device under Chapter 4 (commencing with Section 39080) of Part 1 of Division 26 of the Health and Safety Code unless the motor vehicle is equipped with a certified motor vehicle pollution control device which is correctly installed and in operating condition. No person shall disconnect, modify, or alter any such device in a manner which will decrease its efficiency or effectiveness in the control of air pollution.

Sec. 17. Section 28500 of the Vehicle Code is amended to read:

28500. As used in this chapter:

(a) "Motor vehicle pollution control device" and "certified device" shall be construed as defined in Sections 39093 and 39094 of the Health and Safety Code.

(b) "Station" means a motor vehicle pollution control device installation and inspection station.

(c) "Licensed station" means a station licensed by the department pursuant to this chapter.

(d) "Licensed installer" means a person licensed by the department for installing, repairing, inspecting, or recharging motor vehicle pollution control devices in licensed stations.

Sec. 18. Section 28502 of the Vehicle Code is amended to read:

28502. (a) The department shall license stations and shall designate, furnish instructions to, develop regulations for, and supervise licensed stations for installing, repairing, inspecting, or recharging motor vehicle pollution control devices in conformity with the provisions of Chapter 4 (commencing with Section 39080) of Part 1 of Division 26 of the Health and Safety Code and the rules and regulations of the department. The department shall establish standards for the qualifications, including training, of licensed installers as a condition to designating and licensing the station as a licensed station.

An owner of a fleet of three or more vehicles may be licensed by the department as a licensed station, provided such owner complies with the regulations of the department.

(b) The department shall license, furnish instruction to, develop regulations for, and supervise licensed installers as a condition for installing, repairing, inspecting, or recharging motor vehicle pollution control devices in licensed stations.

Sec. 19. Section 28506 of the Vehicle Code is amended to read:

28506. Any person may install a motor vehicle pollution control device; however, no person who is not a licensed installer shall install such a device for compensation. No such device shall be deemed to meet the requirements of this code or of Chapter 4 (commencing with Section 39080) of Part 1 of Division 26 of the Health and Safety Code and the rules and regulations of the State Air Resources Board unless it has been inspected by a licensed installer in a licensed station and a certificate of compliance has been issued by such licensed station.

Sec. 20. Section 28508 of the Vehicle Code is amended to read:

28508. Whenever a licensed installer in a licensed station, in conformity with the instructions of the department, installs, inspects, repairs, or recharges a motor vehicle pollution control device, and determines that the device conforms with the requirements of Chapter 4 (commencing with Section 39080) of Part 1 of Division 26 of the Health and Safety Code, and the rules and regulations of the State Air Resources Board, a certificate of compliance shall be issued to the owner or driver of the vehicle. The department, for a fee of ten cents ($0.10), shall furnish to the licensed station the certificate of compliance to be issued.

The certificate of compliance shall contain provisions for the date of issuance; the make and registration number of the vehicle; the name of the owner of the vehicle; and the official designation of the station; and if the device involved was approved by the State Air Resources Board by the issuance of a certificate of approval requiring the obtaining of an annual certificate of compliance as authorized by Section 39131 of the Health and Safety Code, a statement that the certificate of compliance shall be valid only through the last day of the 12th month from the date of issuance.

The certificate of compliance shall be signed by a licensed installer who has installed, inspected, repaired, or recharged the motor vehicle pollution control device.

Part 2. Regional Air Pollution Control

CHAPTER 1. GENERAL PROVISIONS

39300. In this part, the terms and definitions contained in Article 1 (commencing with Section 39000), Chapter 1, Part 1, of this division shall apply.

39301. Within each basin established by the board, if the board of supervisors, or respective boards of supervisors, determine there is a need for such a district, or such districts to function, there may be established a regional district for the basin, regional district for a portion of the basin and a county or several county districts, or county districts. No county except a county which on the operative date of this section is within an air pollution control district which is functioning and exercising its powers, shall be required to be represented on a regional board, or have its own board, unless and until the board of supervisors, as authorized by Section 24205 adopt a resolution declaring that there is a need for an air pollution control district to function, or, as authorized by the part, a resolution is adopted by the board of supervisors of the county and by the board of supervisors of one or more other counties declaring there is need for a regional district to function in a common area, including all or any portion of such counties and certified copies of the resolutions are filed with the State Air Resources Board as provided in Section 39354. There shall not be more than one regional air pollution control district in any basin.

39302. The provisions of the Knox-Nisbet Act, Chapter 6.6 (commencing with Section 54773), Part 1, Division 5 of, and the District Reorganization Act of 1965, Division 1 (commencing with Section 56000), Title 6 of, the Government Code shall not be applicable to county districts or regional districts.

CHAPTER 2. DISTRICT AIR POLLUTION
CONTROL BOARDS

39310. The board of supervisors of a county in which a district is not functioning and exercising the powers on the effective date of this part may, pursuant to Chapter 2 (commencing with Section 24198) of Division 20, cause an air pollution control district to commence to function and exercise its powers within the county to carry out the provisions of this division.

A county board of supervisors may establish jointly with other counties in the same basin a regional air pollution control district covering such portion of the county lying within the basin pursuant to this part for purposes of carrying out the provisions of this division.

39311. A county lying within more than one basin may establish jointly with other counties separate regional air pollution control districts and may establish a county air pollution control district for any portion of the county not within a regional district.

39312. If any district organized and functioning pursuant to Chapter 2 (commencing with Section 24198) of Division 20 is entirely within any area in which a regional district is created, upon the establishment of the regional district, such district is dissolved and the regional district succeeds to all of its property and obligations.

39313. Every county district board shall adopt rules and regulations to control the sources of air pollution within the district and shall comply with all the standards, rules and regulations set forth by the state board.

39314. (a) The county district board of any county air pollution control district in existence on the date on which the State Air Resources Board divides the state into basins pursuant to Section 39051, which, on or before such date, has adopted rules and regulations, shall file its rules and regulations with the state board within 30 days after such date.

(b) The county district board of any county air pollution control district in existence on such date which has not, on or before such date, adopted rules and regulations, shall file its rules and regulations with the state board within six months after such date.

(c) The county district board of any county air pollution control district created after such date shall file its rules and regulations with the state board within 12 months after creation of the district.

CHAPTER 3. REGIONAL AIR POLLUTION CONTROL DISTRICTS

Article 1. Creation of Regional Districts

39350. The boards of supervisors of two or more counties within a given basin may upon their own motion, acting separately or shall whenever a petition signed by not less than 10 percent of the qualified electors of each county is presented to the supervisors of that county, hold a public hearing to determine whether or not to become part of a regional air pollution control district.

39351. Prior to the public hearing, the board of supervisors shall give notice of the time and place of hearing by publication pursuant to Section 6061 of the Government Code not less than 15 days nor more than 45 days before such hearing.

39352. Upon conclusion of the public hearing the board of supervisors may adopt a resolution declaring that there is need for the regional district to function in such county, or portion thereof, if from the evidence received at such hearing it finds that it is in the best interests of such county that the regional district function therein.

39353. Upon adoption of the resolution the board of supervisors of such county shall cause a certified copy of it to be filed with the State Air Resources Board.

39354. From and after the date of the filing of certified copies of resolutions from two or more boards desiring a common regional district, the regional district shall begin to function and may exercise its powers within any area not within any other district.

39355. There shall be a separate and distinct city selection committee for each county in which the regional district may transact business and exercise its powers. The membership of such committees shall consist of the mayor of each city within such regional district within the county, which is not within a district, or, where there is no mayor, the chairman or the president of the city council.

39356. A majority of the members of each city selection committee shall constitute a quorum.

39357. The city selection committee for each county shall meet within 90 days after the adoption of the resolution by the board of supervisors to adopt the regional form. The committee of each county shall thereafter meet on the second Monday in May of each even-numbered year, at 10 a.m. in the chambers of the board of supervisors of such county, for the purpose of making succeeding appointments to the regional board as prescribed in Section 39361. At least two weeks prior to the date of each meeting the clerk of the board of supervisors of each county shall give notice of such meeting to each member of the city selection committee of such county. The meeting of the city selection committee of each county shall be conducted in the presence of the clerk of the board of supervisors of such county who shall act as the recording officer for the meeting. It shall be the duty of the clerk of the board of supervisors to notify in writing the board of supervisors of such county and also the clerk of the regional board of the appointment made by the city selection committee within 10 days after such appointment has been made.

39358. Each committee shall appoint a chairman from among its members and such other officers as may be necessary.

39359. Members of the committees shall serve without compensation, but may be allowed actual expenses incurred in the discharge of their duties.

39360. The board of supervisors of a county in which the regional district may transact business and exercise its powers shall appoint one of its members to be a member of the regional board.

The selection committee of each county shall appoint one member of the regional board. Such member shall be selected from among the mayors and city councilmen of the cities within such county.

39361. Members of a newly created regional board selected by a city selection committee and a board of supervisors shall serve terms which shall expire on the first day of June of the third year following the year in which they are appointed. Thereafter terms of the regional board members appointed by the board of supervisors shall be for four years and until the appointment and qualification of his successor and each member appointed by the city selection committee shall hold office for two years and until the appointment and qualification of his successor. Any vacancy on the regional board shall be filled by appointment in the same manner as the vacating member was appointed. Any member of the regional board may be removed at any time in the same manner as he was appointed; provided, however, that if four-fifths of the members of the board of supervisors of a county request the removal of a member appointed by the city selection committee of such county, the city selection committee of such county shall meet within 20 days to consider the removal of such member.

39362. Any member of the regional board may be recalled from his office of member of the board of supervisors or of mayor or member of the legislative body of a city pursuant to Division 13 of the Elections Code, in which event his office as member of the regional board shall be vacant.

39363. The regional board is the governing body of the regional district and shall exercise all the powers of the regional district, except as otherwise provided.

39364. A majority of the members of the regional board constitutes a quorum for the transaction of business and may act for the regional board.

39365. Each member of the regional board shall receive the actual and necessary expenses incurred by him in the performance of his duties, plus a compensation of twenty-five dollars ($25) for each day attending the meetings of the board, but such compensation shall not exceed six hundred dollars ($600) in any one year.

39366. The regional board may appoint an executive secretary to perform such duties as may be assigned to him by the board.

39367. The regional board may cooperate and contract with any federal, state, or local governmental agencies, private industries, or civic groups necessary or proper to the accomplishment of the purposes of this chapter.

39368. No supervisor, mayor, or city councilman shall hold office on the regional board for a period of more than three months after ceasing to hold the office of supervisor, mayor, or city councilman, respectively, and his membership on the regional board shall thereafter be considered vacant, except that any mayor who continues to hold office as a city councilman, or city councilman who continues to hold office as mayor, shall not be considered to have ceased to hold office under this section.

Article 2. Powers and Duties

39380. The regional district shall have power:

(a) To have perpetual succession.

(b) To sue and be sued in the name of the regional district in all actions and proceedings in all courts and tribunals of competent jurisdiction.

(c) To adopt a seal and alter it at its pleasure.

(d) To take by grant, purchase, gift, devise, or lease, hold, use, enjoy, and to lease or dispose of real or personal property of every kind within or without the regional district necessary to the full exercise of its powers.

(e) To lease, sell or dispose of any property or any interest therein whenever in the judgment of the regional board such property, or any interest therein, or part thereof, is no longer required for the purposes of the regional district, or may be leased for any purpose without interfering with the use of the same for the purposes of the regional district, and to pay any compensation received therefor into the general fund of the regional district.

39381. The regional district shall establish and execute an effective program for the reduction of air contaminants within the regional district and shall enforce all orders, rules and regulations prescribed by the state board relating to the sources of air pollution within its jurisdiction.

39382. The regional district shall do such acts as may be necessary to carry out the provisions of this chapter.

39383. The regional board shall establish and maintain such offices wherever it deems will best facilitate the accomplishment of the regional objectives.

39384. The regional board shall meet at such times and places as decided by the regional board.

39385. The regional board shall appoint a chairman from its members and such other officers as may be necessary.

39386. The regional board shall determine the compensation of, any pay from regional district funds, the control officer, all of his personnel, the executive secretary, and members of the hearing board.

39387. The regional board shall provide for the number of personnel to be employed by the control officer and for their duties and the times at which they shall be appointed.

39388. The regional board may contract with any city or county, any state department, or any competent person or agency for the conducting of competitive examinations to ascertain the fitness of applicants for employment and for the performance of any other service in connection with administration of the regional district.

39389. The regional board may by ordinance adopt a civil service system for any or all employees of the regional district except that the executive secretary and air pollution control officer shall be exempt from such system and shall serve at the pleasure of the regional board. The board may adopt regulations and bylaws for the organization and administration of the regional district and may, in such regulations, provide for amendment and repeal thereof.

39390. In exercising its powers and duties, the regional district shall, whenever feasible, secure necessary technical, administrative and operational services by contract with public agencies to the end that duplication of similar services and facilities is avoided to the extent possible. This section shall not be construed as requiring the regional board to contract for services which the board determines should, in the best interests of the regional district, be provided by the regional district or services which can be provided by the regional district at a lesser cost than by contract.

Article 3. Air Pollution Control Officer

39400. The regional board shall appoint an air pollution control officer.

39401. Subject to the provisions of Article 2 (commencing with Section 39380) of this chapter, the control officer shall appoint his personnel.

39402. The control officer shall observe and enforce:

(a) The provisions of this chapter.

(b) All orders, regulations, and rules prescribed by the regional board.

(c) All variances and standards which the regional hearing board has prescribed.

Article 4. Advisory Council

39410. The regional board may appoint an air pollution control advisory council to advise and consult with the regional board and the control officer in effectuating the purposes of this chapter. The council shall consist of the chairman of the regional board, who shall serve as an ex officio member, and members who preferably are skilled and experienced in the field of air pollution, and a representative of the academic community, health agencies, agriculture, industry, community planning, transportation, registered professional engineers, general contractors, architects, and organized labor.

39411. The council shall select a chairman and vice chairman and such other officers as it deems necessary.

39412. Council members shall serve without compensation but may be allowed actual expenses incurred in the discharge of their duties. The council shall meet as frequently as the board or the council deem necessary.

Article 5. Hearing Board

39420. Within 30 days after the regional district, by resolution, determines it necessary to adopt rules and regulations to control the release of air contaminants, the regional board shall appoint a hearing board, to consist of three members, none of whom is otherwise employed by the district. One member shall have been admitted to practice law in this state. One member shall be registered as a professional engineer in California and experienced in the field of air pollution control.

39421. The regional board shall appoint one member of the hearing board for a term of one year, one for a term of two years, and one for a term of three years. Thereafter the terms of members of the hearing board shall be three years.

Article 6. Enforcement

39430. A person shall not discharge from any source whatsoever such quantities of air contaminants, smoke, or other material which cause injury, detriment, nuisance or annoyance to any considerable number of persons or to the public or which endanger the comfort, repose, health or safety of any such persons or the public or which cause or have a natural tendency to cause injury or damage to business or property.

39431. This article does not apply to smoke from fire set by or permitted by any public officer if such fire is set or permission given in the performance of the official duty of such officer, for the purpose of weed abatement, the prevention of a fire hazard, or the instruction of public employees in the methods of fighting fire, which is, in the opinion of such officer, necessary.

39432. This article does not apply to:

(a) Smoke from fires set by, or permitted by, the county agricultural commissioner of any county within the regional district for agricultural operations in the growing of crops or raising of fowl or animals, if such fire is set or permission given in the performance of the official duty of such county agricultural commissioner, except that such fires shall not be set or permission given in violation of any general order, rule, or regulation adopted by the regional board pursuant to Section 39463.

(b) Smoke from fires set by, or permitted by, the State Forester or his agent for the purpose of watershed, range, or pasture improvement if such fire is set or permission given in the performance of the official duty of the State Forester or his agent, except that such fires shall not be set or permission given in violation of any general order, rule, or regulation adopted by the regional board pursuant to Section 39463.

39433. The Legislature does not, by the provisions of this chapter, intend to occupy the field.

The provisions of this chapter do not prohibit the enactment or enforcement by any county or city of any local ordinance more restrictive than, or identical to, the provisions of this article and more restrictive than, or identical to, the rules and regulations adopted pursuant to this chapter, which local ordinance prohibits, regulates or controls air pollution.

Counties and cities may, by local ordinance, provide for the local enforcement of this article and of regulations adopted pursuant to this chapter.

39434. The provisions of this chapter do not supersede any such local county or city ordinance.

39435. If it should be held that provisions of this chapter supersede the provisions of any local county or city ordinance, such suspension shall not bar the prosecution or punishment of any violation of such ordinance which violation was committed when such ordinance was in full force and effect.

39436. Nothing in this article limits in any way the power of the regional board to make needful orders, rules, and regulations pursuant to other provisions of this chapter. Nothing in this article permits any action contrary to any such order, rule, or regulation.

39437. Any violation of any provisions of this article or of any order, rule, or regulation of the regional board may be enjoined in a civil action brought in the name of the people of the State of California.

39438. Every person who violates any provision of this article or any order, rule, or regulation of the regional board is guilty of a misdemeanor.

Every day during any portion of which such violation occurs constitutes a separate offense.

39439. The provisions of Section 39430 relating to odors do not apply to odors emanating from agricultural operations in the growing of crops or raising of fowls or animals.

39440. Except as provided in Sections 39431 and 39432, orders, rules, and regulations of the regional board shall apply to every state agency, governmental subdivision, district, public and quasi-public corporation, public agency, and public service corporation, and every city, county, city and county, and municipal corporation.

Article 7. Rules and Regulations

39460. The regional board shall adopt and may, from time to time, amend rules and regulations, including, but not limited to, rules and regulations establishing standards to implement this chapter. Such rules and regulations shall be based on surveys and studies made by the regional district and such other information as may be available to the regional district. The rules and regulations shall be adopted only after the regional board has considered the matter at a public hearing at which all interested persons are afforded the opportunity to appear and urge or oppose adoption of the resolution. The regional board shall give notice of its intention to adopt or amend rules and regulations and give notice of the hearing by publication pursuant to Section 6061 of the Government Code in each of the counties within the regional district not less than 10 days prior to the hearing. The notice shall contain the time and place of the hearing and such other information as may be necessary to reasonably apprise the people within the regional district of the nature and purpose of the meeting. The hearing may be adjourned from time to time in order to permit presentation of all pertinent testimony.

39461. (a) The regional board of any regional district in existence on the date on which the State Air Resources Board divides the state into basins pursuant to Section 39051, which, on or before such dates, has adopted rules and regulations, shall file its rules and regulations with the state board within 30 days after such dates.

(b) The regional board of any regional district in existence on such date which has not, on or before such date, adopted rules and regulations, shall file its rules and regulations with the state board within six months after such date.

(c) The regional board of any regional district created after such date shall file its rules and regulations with the state board within 12 months after creation of the district.

39462. A city, county or city and county may adopt orders, rules, or regulations which may be more restrictive than those adopted by a regional board.

39463. Whenever the regional board finds that the air in the regional district is so polluted as to cause discomfort or property damage at intervals to a substantial number of inhabitants of the region, the regional board may make, in accordance with the procedures prescribed in this article, and may enforce such general orders, rules, and regulations as will reduce the amount of air contaminants released within the regional district.

39464. The control officer at any time may require from any person subject to regulations of the regional board, such information or analyses as will disclose the nature, extent, quantity, or degree of air contaminants which are or may be discharged by such source, and may require that such disclosures be certified by a professional engineer registered in the State. In addition to such report, the control officer may designate and employ a registered professional engineer of his choice to make an independent study and report as to the nature, extent, quantity, and degree of any air contaminants which are or may be discharged from the source. An engineer so designated is authorized to inspect any article, machine, equipment or other contrivance necessary to make the inspection and report.

39465. If any person within a reasonable time willfully fails or refuses to furnish to the control officer information or analyses requested by such control officer, or if the control officer finds that any order, rule, or regulation of the regional board is being violated after a reasonable time has been allowed for compliance, the control officer shall notify the hearing board of such facts and request a public hearing on the matter.

39466. Within 30 days after the control officer has requested a public hearing, the hearing board shall hold such a hearing and give notice of the time and place of such hearing to the person cited, to the control officer and to such other persons as the hearing board deems should be notified, not less than 10 days before the date of the public hearing.

39467. After a public hearing, the hearing board may find that no violation exists, or may take any of the actions provided in Article 8 and Article 9 of this chapter.

Article 8. Variances

39470. The provisions of this chapter do not prohibit the discharge of air contaminants to a greater extent or for a longer time, or both, than permitted by Article 6 or by rules, regulations, or orders of the regional board, if not of a greater extent or longer time than the hearing board or a court after a hearing before the hearing board finds necessary pursuant to the provisions of this article.

39471. The hearing board on its own motion or at the request of any person may hold a hearing to determine under what conditions and to what extent a variance from the requirements established by Article 6 or by rules, regulations, or orders of the regional board is necessary and will be permitted.

39472. The regional board may provide, by regulation, a schedule of fees which will yield a sum not exceeding the estimated cost of the administration of this article, for the filing of applications for variances or to revoke or modify variances. All applicants shall pay the fees required by such regulations.

39473. All such fees shall be paid to the regional district treasurer to the credit of the regional district.

39474. The hearing board shall serve a notice of the time and place of a hearing to grant a variance upon the control officer and upon the applicant, if any, not less than 10 days prior to such hearing.

39475. If the hearing board finds that because of conditions beyond control compliance with Article 6 or with any rule, regulation, or order of the regional board will result in an arbitrary and unreasonable taking of property or in the practical closing and elimination of any lawful business, occupation or activity, in either case without a sufficient corresponding benefit or advantage to the people in the reduction of air contamination, it shall prescribe other and different requirements not more onerous applicable to plants and equipment operated either by named classes of industries or persons, or to the operation of separate persons; provided, however, that no variance may permit or authorize the maintenance of a nuisance.

39476. In determining under what conditions and to what extent a variance from said requirements is necessary and will be permitted, the hearing board shall exercise a wide discretion in weighing the equities involved and the advantages and disadvantages to the residents of the regional district and to any lawful business, occupation or activity involved, resulting from requiring compliance with said requirements or resulting from granting a variance.

39477. The hearing board may revoke or modify by written order, after a public hearing held upon not less than 10 days' notice, any order permitting a variance.

39478. The hearing board shall serve notice of the time and place of a hearing to revoke or modify any order permitting a variance not less than 10 days prior to such hearing upon the control officer, upon all persons who will be subjected to greater restrictions if such order is revoked or modified as proposed and upon all other persons interested or likely to be affected who have filed with the hearing board or control officer a written request for such notification.

39479. The hearing board shall serve a notice of the time and place of a hearing to grant a variance or to revoke or modify an order permitting a variance either by personal service or by first-class mail, postage prepaid. If either the identity or address of any person entitled to notice is unknown, the hearing board shall serve such person by publication of notice in the district pursuant to Section 6061 of the Government Code.

39480. The hearing board in making any order permitting a variance may specify the time during which such order will be effective, in no event to exceed one year, but such variance may be continued from year to year without another hearing on the approval of the control officer.

39481. If any local county or city ordinance has provided regulations similar to those in Article 6 or to any order, regulation, or rule prescribed by the regional board, and has provided for the granting of variances, and pursuant to such local ordinance a variance has been granted prior to notification of the regional district, such variance shall be continued as a variance of the hearing board for the time specified therein or one year, whichever is shorter, or until and unless prior to the expiration of such time the hearing board modifies or revokes such variance as provided in this article.

Article 9. Procedure

39490. This article applies to all hearings which this chapter provides shall be held by the hearing board.

39491. The hearing board shall select from its number a chairman.

39492. The hearing board may hold a hearing in bank or may designate two or one of their number to hold a hearing.

39493. If two or three members of the hearing board conduct a hearing the concurrence of two shall be necessary to a decision.

39494. The hearing board, not less than two being present, may, in its discretion, within 30 days rehear any matter which was decided by a single member.

39495. Whenever the members of the hearing board conducting any hearing deem it necessary to examine any person as a witness at such hearing, the chairman of the hearing board shall issue a subpoena, in proper form, commanding such person to appear before it at a time and place specified to be examined as a witness. The subpoena may require such person to produce all books, papers, and documents in his possession or under his control material to such hearing.

39496. A subpoena to appear before the hearing board shall be served in the same manner as a subpoena in a civil action.

39497. Whenever any person duly subpoenaed to appear and give evidence or to produce any books and papers before the hearing board neglects or refuses to appear, or to produce any books and papers, as required by the subpoena, or refuses to testify or to answer any question which the hearing board decides is proper and pertinent, he shall be deemed in contempt, and the hearing board shall report the fact to the judge of the superior court of the county in which the person resides.

39498. Upon receipt of the report, the judge of the superior court shall issue an attachment directed to the sheriff of the county where the witness was required to appear and testify, commanding the sheriff to attach such person and forthwith bring him before the judge who ordered the attachment issued.

39499. On the return of the attachment and the production of the body of the defendant, the judge has jurisdiction of the matter. The person charged may purge himself of the contempt in the same way, and the same proceeding shall be had, and the same penalties may be imposed, and the same punishment inflicted as in the case of a witness subpoenaed to appear and give evidence on the trial of a civil cause before a superior court.

39500. Every member of the hearing board may administer oaths in every hearing in which he participates, and at any hearing the hearing board may require all or any witnesses to be sworn before testifying.

39501. The hearing board may adopt rules for the conduct of its hearings not inconsistent with this chapter. Such rules shall so far as practicable conform to the rules for administrative adjudication by state agencies in Chapter 5 (commencing with Section 11500) of Part 1 of Division 3 of Title 2 of the Government Code.

Article 10. Enforcement

39502. Whenever the hearing board finds that any person is in violation of Section 39430, Section 39434, or any order, rule, or regulation of the regional board, and that no variance is justified and that a reasonable time has been allowed for compliance, the hearing board shall make a decision setting forth findings of fact and such conclusions of law as are required in view of the issues submitted. The decision shall contain an order for abatement. The order for abatement shall be framed in the manner of a writ of injunction requiring the respondent to refrain from a particular act. The order may be conditional and require a respondent to refrain from a particular act unless certain conditions are met. The order shall not have the effect of permitting a variance unless all the conditions for a variance, including limitation of time, are met.

39503. The hearing board shall announce its decision in the form of a draft before filing. Copies of the draft shall be mailed to the parties or their attorneys. The hearing board may direct the prevailing party to prepare a form of decision. Any party may file objections to the draft with the hearing board within 10 days after mailing.

39504. After objections, if any, have been considered by the hearing board or a hearing has been held thereon, if the hearing board finds it necessary, the hearing board shall file its decision with its clerk, who shall give notice of such filing to the parties or their attorneys.

39505. The decision shall become effective 30 days after it is filed unless:

(a) A rehearing is granted by the hearing board.

(b) The hearing board orders that it be made effective sooner.

39506. Judicial review may be had by filing a petition for a writ of mandate in accordance with the provisions of the Code of Civil Procedure. Except as otherwise provided in this section, any such petition shall be filed within 30 days after the last day on which reconsideration can be ordered. The right to petition shall not be affected by the failure to seek reconsideration before the hearing board. The complete record of the proceedings, or such parts thereof as are designated by the petitioner, shall be prepared by the hearing board and shall be delivered to the petitioner within 30 days after a request therefor by him, upon payment of the fees specified in Section 69950 of the Government Code, as now or hereinafter amended, for the transcript, the cost of preparation of other portions of the record, and for certification thereof. The complete record includes the pleadings, all notices and orders issued by the hearing board, any proposed decision by the hearing board, the final decision, a transcript of all proceedings, the exhibits admitted or rejected, the written evidence and any other papers in the case. Where petitioner, within 10 days after the last day on which reconsideration can be ordered, requests the hearing board to prepare all or any part of the record, the time within which a petition may be filed shall be extended until five days after its delivery to him. The hearing board may file with the court the original of any document in the record in lieu of a copy thereof.

39507. In any proceeding pursuant to Section 39506, the court shall receive in evidence any order, rule, or regulation of the board, any transcript of the proceedings before the hearing board, and such further evidence as the court in its discretion deems proper.

39508. A proceeding for mandatory or prohibitory injunction shall be brought by the district in the name of the people of the State of California in the superior court of the county in which the violation occurs to enjoin any person to whom an order for abatement pursuant to Section 39502 has been directed and who violates such order.

39509. Proceedings under Section 39508 shall conform to the requirements of Chapter 3 (commencing with Section 525) of Title 7 of Part 2 of the Code of Civil Procedure, except that it shall not be necessary to show lack of adequate remedy at law or to show irreparable damages or loss. In any such proceeding, it shall be shown that an order for abatement has been made, that it has become final, and that its operation has not been stayed, it shall be sufficient proof to warrant the granting of a preliminary injunction. If in addition it shall be shown that the respondent continues or threatens to continue to violate such order for abatement, it shall be sufficient proof to warrant the immediate granting of a temporary restraining order.

Article 11. Financial Provisions

39520. The regional district may borrow money and incur indebtedness in anticipation of the revenue for the current year in which the indebtedness is incurred or of the ensuing year. Such indebtedness shall not exceed the total amount of the estimate of the tax income for either the current year of the ensuing year.

39521. Before the 15th day of June of each year the regional board shall estimate and determine the amount of money required by the regional district for purposes of the regional district during the ensuing fiscal year and shall apportion this amount to the counties included within the regional district, one-half according to the relative value of the real estate of each county within the regional district as determined by the regional board and one-half in the proportion that the population of each county within the regional district bears to the total population of the regional district. For the purposes of this Section, the regional board shall base its determination of the population of the several counties on the latest official information available to it.

39522. On or before the 15th day of June of each year, the regional board shall inform the board of supervisors of each county of the amount apportioned to the county. Each board of supervisors shall levy an ad valorem tax on the taxable property, but not including intangible personal property, within the county included within the regional district sufficient to secure the amount so apportioned to it and such taxes shall be levied and collected together with, and not separately from, the taxes for county purposes and paid to the treasurer of each of the counties to the credit of the regional district.

39523. Taxes levied by the board of supervisors for the benefit of the regional district shall be a lien upon all property within such county lying within the regional district and shall have the same force and effect as other liens for taxes. Their collection may be enforced in the same manner as liens for county taxes are enforced.

39524. At any time prior to the first receipt by the regional district of revenues from taxation, the counties within the regional district may loan any available money to the region for purposes of organization and operation and such expenditures shall constitute a proper expenditure of county funds. The regional board shall add the sums of money so borrowed from the counties to the first amount apportioned by the board pursuant to Section 39521, and shall repay the counties for all money borrowed from the first revenues received from taxation.

39525. The treasurers of the several counties within the region shall pay into the regional district treasury all funds held by them to the credit of the regional district.

39526. The regional district treasury shall be in the custody of the county treasurer of a county in the regional district designated by the regional board and such treasurer shall be the regional district treasurer.

39527. The regional board shall, in carrying out the provisions of this article, comply as nearly as possible with the provisions of Chapter 1 (commencing with Section 29000) of Division 3 of Title 3 of the Government Code.

Article 12. Withdrawal of County from Regional District

39540. The board of supervisors of a county within a regional district may upon the adoption of a resolution stating such, withdraw from the regional district and establish its own county air pollution control district.

The resolution so adopted shall be communicated to the clerks of the boards of supervisors of all counties comprising the regional district, the regional board, and the Air Resources Board.

39541. The withdrawal of a county shall not affect the functioning of other counties within the regional district, and such withdrawal shall not constitute a dissolution of the regional district.

The regional district shall continue to function in a manner not inconsistent with the provisions of this part.

39542. A regional district may be dissolved in a manner which conforms to Section 24372.

39543. A county shall give at least two months' notice to the regional board of its intention to withdraw from the regional district. A county shall not be withdrawn from a regional district during any fiscal year after the expiration of the first four months of such fiscal year.

Article 13. Claims

39560. All claims for money or damages against the regional district are governed by Part 3 (commencing with Section 900) and Part 4 (commencing with Section 940) of Division 3.6 of Title 1 of the Government Code except as provided therein, or by other statutes or regulations expressly applicable thereto.

Article 14. Bay Area Pollution Control District

39570. The Bay Area Pollution Control District created pursuant to Chapter 2.5 (commencing with Section 24345) of Division 20 and Humboldt County shall be exempt from the provisions of this part.

Sec. 6. There is hereby appropriated from the General Fund the sum of one hundred thousand dollars ($100,000) to the State Air Resources Board for expenditure by the board during the 1967-68 fiscal year in carrying out the provisions of Part 1 (commencing with Section 39000) of Division 26 of the Health and Safety Code as enacted by Section 5 of this Act.

Sec. 7. This Act shall be known as the Mulford-Carrell Act.

Model State Air Pollution Control Act

Suggested legislation for a state air pollution control act has been developed by the Committee of State Officials on Suggested State Legislation, of the Council of State Governments.

The Council made the following statement about the model law:

> The declaration of policy provided by Section 1 of the suggested Act is of greater importance than similar provisions often appearing in statutes, because the considerations set forth in the declaration are later used in various parts of the legislation as legislative standards to be taken into account by the administering agency in making its rules and regulations and in issuing orders.

> The question of administrative organization for air pollution control is one to which no single approach can be taken with confidence that it is superior in all cases. The board or commission has been used to a considerable extent by those jurisdictions with air pollution control statutes or ordinances, because it offers a familiar means of encouraging the examination and representation of different points of view and interests in the policy making process and in the making of determinations that some would consider quasi-legislative and quasi-judicial. In addition, advisory committees representing interested parties, technical and professional groups and the general public have also been established in the air pollution field. On the other hand, the regular departmental type of organization is widely used in many regulatory programs and is generally held to provide certain advantages in efficiency of operation and orderly administration. The suggested legislation includes four alternatives for administrative organization. One would place the activity within an existing state department; another provides for a commission made up of the heads of existing state agencies with relevant program responsibilities and local government representatives; still another provides for a mixed commission composed in part of state officials and in part of representation from technical and interest groups outside state government. The alternative listed as number two in the suggested legislation would be a combination of the departmental

approach for administration with the mixed commission device for the making of rules and regulations. Yet another possibility which is not represented by draft language but which could be employed consistently with the provisions of the suggested legislation is the establishment of an entirely separate department of state government for air pollution control, rather than the placing of the air pollution control agency within an existing department. An "Advisory Council" consisting of interest group and technical representation is included as part of the first and third alternatives. It is omitted from the other two because of the composition of the commission itself. The other sections of the Act are so drafted as to fit with whichever pattern of administrative organization is selected. It should be noted that to date the customary practice has been to assign air pollution control responsibilities to the Health Department or to connect the air pollution control agency more closely to that Department than to any other unit of state government. However, the decision as to the location of the function in state government may be made differently in different jurisdictions and no effort is made here to judge among the possible choices.

The entire subject of administrative organization of the state agency was considered of great importance by the members of the advisory group that assisted in the preparation of the suggested legislation. The key problem is presented by the nature of the governmental agency having responsibility in this field. Some of the officials and organizations represented were strongly of the opinion that only persons who are full time public officials should have the responsibility for making and administering public policy. In this view, the only proper place for representatives of private interests is on an advisory body. Others contended that the imperfect state of knowledge in the air pollution field and the need to balance the interests of the large number of social and economic interests involved makes air pollution control a particularly appropriate field for the employment of a mixed commission, consisting of public officials and representatives of the affected groups in the private sector. Preferences among the four organizational alternatives presented in Section 3 of the suggested Act undoubtedly will be determined in part by the reader's appraisal of the merits of these competing points of view.

Section 5 authorizes reporting for such classes of contaminant sources as may be necessary and desirable after due consideration of health, social and economic factors, and physical effects on property. Meaningful surveillance of air quality essential for determining the nature of problems in statewide or regional air basins and for fashioning control programs appropriate to each basin may benefit from such authority. The section, it should be noted, would provide for reporting by contaminant sources only of such information as may be reasonably available.

In connection with the construction or installation of new air contaminant sources, Section 6 allows the state agency to require the use of available methods, devices, or construction features known to prevent or significantly reduce emissions. The state agency could require the submission of plans, specifications, and related information.

The authority conferred by this section is intended primarily for use in those situations where it may be found that differing methods of construction or equipping of facilities are economically reasonable, but where it may be desirable to require that choice among them which best prevents or reduces air pollution.

The next to the last item in Section 4 on Powers, it should be added, provides for agency consultation on request with those proposing to acquire or construct installations concerning air pollution problems and the adequacy of control systems which may be involved.

Under Section 8 the state agency could establish source emission limits for the state as a whole or varying with areas in the state so as to reflect the purposes of the Act and differing local conditions. Correlative local control program requirements must be at least as stringent. Elsewhere in the Act, the state agency is given power to develop and issue ambient air standards.

For those rare circumstances when human health or safety is endangered by intensive air pollution incidents, Section 10 authorizes the agency Director, with the concurrence of the Governor, to order any sources to reduce or discontinue forthwith contaminant emissions. Such order would be followed within twenty-four hours by a hearing before the state agency and the order affirmed, modified, or set aside.

The state agency under Section 11 may provide for variances if the discharges thereby allowed do not endanger human health or safety and if compliance with regulations governing emissions would produce serious hardships without countervailing public benefits. No variance may be allowed except after public hearing and until the relative interests of the applicant, the public, and other property owners likely to be affected are considered.

Section 14 would mandate air pollution programs in larger municipalities and counties. Such local operations would be subject to state agency approval as having:

a. Requirements compatible with or stricter or more extensive than those of the state under Sections 8, 10, and 11 for emission controls, emergency procedures, and variances respectively;

b. Appropriate administrative and judicial processes as well as suitable staff and other resources; and

c. A program adequate to meet the requirements of the Act and any applicable rules and regulations.

Local governments of lesser population than those with mandated programs could, if they chose, opt to establish their own air pollution operations subject to the same requirements. Joint local programs, whether for part or for the entire function, are encouraged and indeed may be mandated if it is found necessary for effective control of air pollution problems.

A State Aid section, for which detail necessary to establish a program of assistance must be spelled out, would provide for grants equal to 30 per cent of the locally funded operating costs of a local air pollution control program, and 50 per cent of the correlative locally funded share of the cost of operations of interlocal air pollution control activity.

Section 16 deals with the control of pollution from motor vehicles. Since Congress has provided for the setting of construction and equipment requirements on new vehicles (beginning with the 1968 models), this section provides that the state shall not require inspection, certification or approval of any federally prescribed features or equipment, prior to initial sale of the vehicle. The section also recognizes that state regulation of pollution from motor vehicles must be consistent with the state of the art and technology. Within this context, the section provides for the inspection of vehicular air pollution control mechanisms or features, as part of the regular state motor vehicle inspection program. Vehicles not found to be in good order in this respect would be denied inspection stickers and would be subject to cancellation of registration, until the defects were remedied. The state air pollution control agency would be required to provide the state motor vehicle agency with the technical knowledge and instruction necessary to permit it to discharge its inspection responsibilities.

There are some existing air pollution control programs that make use of an Appeals Board as a first avenue of review for those dissatisfied with the actions of the air pollution control administrator. Such a device, as an intermediate stage between administrative action and litigation may be desirable, if an Appeals Board can be devised that is both impartial and knowledgeable in the field of air pollution control. One view is that an Appeals Board also can be useful, particularly where the air pollution control agency does not contain representation from affected interest groups. However, in view of the wide variety of patterns for administrative organization presented as alternatives in the suggested Act and the uneven relevance of possible Appeals Board machinery to each of the several alternatives, no effort has been made to include a provision on this subject.

The suggested legislation also contains provisions for enforcement, confidentiality of certain information, judicial review, and penalties.

Suggested Legislation

[Title should conform to state requirements. The following is a suggestion: "An Act providing for the conservation of the air quality of the State; the prevention, abatement and control of air pollution and for related purposes."]

(Be it enacted, etc.)

SECTION 1. DECLARATION OF POLICY AND PURPOSE

(a) It is hereby declared to be the public policy of this State and the purpose of this Act to achieve and maintain such levels of air quality as will protect human health and safety, and to the greatest degree practicable, prevent injury to plant and animal life and property, foster the comfort and convenience of the people, promote the economic and social development of this State and facilitate the enjoyment of the natural attractions of this State.

(b) It is also declared that local and regional air pollution control programs are to be supported to the extent practicable as essential instruments for the securing and maintenance of appropriate levels of air quality.

(c) To these ends it is the purpose of this Act to provide for a coordinated statewide program of air pollution prevention, abatement and control; for an appropriate distribution of responsibilities among the state and local units of government; to facilitate cooperation across jurisdictional lines in dealing with problems of air pollution not confined within single jurisdictions; and to provide a framework within which all values may be balanced in the public interest.

SECTION 2. DEFINITIONS

As used in this Act:

(a) "Air contaminant" means dust, fumes, mist, smoke, other particulate matter, vapor, gas, odorous substances, or any combination thereof.

(b) "Air pollution" means the presence in the outdoor atmosphere of one or more air contaminants in such quantities and duration as is or tends to be injurious to human health or welfare, animal or plant life, or property, or would unreasonably interfere with the enjoyment of life or property.

(c) "Emission" means a release into the outdoor atmosphere of air contaminants.

(d) "Person" means any individual, partnership, firm, association, municipality, public or private corporation, subdivision or agency of the State, trust, estate or any other legal entity.

ALTERNATE I

SECTION 3. DIVISION OF AIR POLLUTION CONTROL; ADVISORY COUNCIL

(a) There is hereby created a Division of Air Pollution Control, hereinafter referred to as "the Division," in the [Department of Health]. The [Department of Health] shall administer this Act through the Division, which shall be headed by a Director appointed by the head of the [Department].

(b) There is hereby created an Air Pollution Control Advisory Council, hereinafter referred to as "the Advisory Council," of [fifteen] members to be appointed by the Governor, including [one] registered professional engineer experienced and competent in matters of air pollution control; [one] licensed physician knowledgeable in the health effects of air pollution; [one] urban or regional planner; [one] representing the power generating industry; [one] representing the fuels industry; [one] representing the manufacturing components of industry; [one] representing agriculture; [one] representing conservation; [one] representing county government; [one] representing municipal government; [one] representing labor; and [four] appointed at large. Such administrative services and monies as may be made available to or for the Advisory Council shall be charges on the Division.

(c) The Director shall serve as secretary of the Advisory Council. The Advisory Council shall annually select a chairman from among its members.

(d) Members of the Advisory Council shall serve at the pleasure of the Governor: provided that no member representing subdivisions of the State may continue in such capacity except during the time when he is an official or employee of a municipality, county, or interlocal agency of municipalities or counties. The members shall be compensated [at the rate of [$] per day when engaged on business of the Advisory Council] [in accordance with state law].

(e) The Advisory Council shall consider rules and regulations as provided in Section 12, and any other matters related to the purposes of the Act submitted to it by the Division; and may make recommendations on its own initiative to the Division concerning the administration of this Act. The Advisory Council shall meet at the call of the Director or at the written request of [five] members.

(f) In addition to its regular employees, the Division may employ such consultants as may be appropriate.

ALTERNATE II

SECTION 3. DIVISION OF AIR POLLUTION CONTROL; COMMISSION

(a) There is hereby created a Division of Air Pollution Control, hereinafter referred to as "the Division," in the [Department of Health].

The [Department of Health] shall administer this Act through the Division, which shall be headed by a Director appointed by the head of the [Department]: provided that rules and regulations required or authorized to be made pursuant to this Act shall be made, amended and repealed by the Air Pollution Control Commission established pursuant to subsection (b) of this Section.

    (b) [Same as subsection (a) of Alternate IV below.]
    (c) [Same as subsection (b) of Alternate IV below.]
    (d) [Same as subsection (c) of Alternate IV below.]
    (e) [Same as subsection (d) of Alternate IV below.]
    (f) [Same as subsection (f) of Alternate I above.]

ALTERNATE III

SECTION 3. AIR POLLUTION CONTROL COMMISSION; ADVISORY COUNCIL

(a) There is hereby created the Air Pollution Control Commission, hereinafter referred to as "the Commission."[1] The members of the Commission shall be the heads of the Departments of [Health, Commerce, Labor, Conservation and Agriculture],[2] and two other members, appointed by the Governor, [serving terms of [ ] years], representing respectively county and municipal government. No member representing county or municipal government may continue in such capacity except during the time when he is an official or employee of a county, municipality or interlocal governmental agency, as the case may be. Whenever a vacancy occurs, the Governor shall appoint a member for the remaining portion of the unexpired term created by the vacancy. The Commission shall select annually a chairman from among its members.

(b) The Commission shall hold at least four regular meetings each year and such additional meetings as the chairman deems desirable, at a place and time to be fixed by the chairman. Special meetings shall be called by the chairman upon written request of any three members. Four members shall constitute a quorum. The heads of the Departments of [Health, Commerce, Labor, Conservation and Agriculture] each may designate a principal deputy or assistant to act in his place and stead on the Commission.

(c) In accordance with the [state merit system law], the Commission shall appoint a Director of Air Pollution Control, hereinafter referred to as "the Director," who shall be the principal administrative officer of the Commission. The Commission shall provide by rules and regulations consistent with law for the performance by its officers and employees, in the name of the Commission, of any act or duty necessary or incidental to the administration of this Act.

(d) The Commission may employ such personnel and consultants as may be necessary for the administration of this Act. Subject to any appli-

---

   [1] The Commission may be established as an independent agency but could be placed within an existing state department for housekeeping purposes. In any event, it is important that statutory authority flow directly to the Commission and that it have independent powers.

   [2] If a state agency other than those named is charged by law with an aspect of the air pollution control program (e.g. the motor vehicle agency with respect to vehicular pollution), consideration should be given to including such agency.

cable restrictions contained in law, any department or agency of the State may from its available resources provide the Commission with personnel and services, with or without charge. The Commission may compensate such other agencies for services.

(e) There is hereby established an Air Pollution Control Advisory Council, hereinafter referred to as "the Advisory Council," of [thirteen] members to be appointed by the Governor including [one] registered professional engineer experienced and competent in matters of air pollution control; [one] licensed physician knowledgeable in the health effects of air pollution; [one] urban or regional planner; [one] representing the power generating industry; [one] representing the fuels industry; [one] representing the manufacturing components of industry; [one] representing agriculture; [one] representing conservation; [one] representing labor; and [four] appointed at large. The Director shall serve as secretary of the Advisory Council. Such administrative services and monies as may be made available to or for the Advisory Council shall be charges on the Commission.

(f) Members of the Advisory Council shall serve at the pleasure of the Governor. The members shall be compensated [at the rate of [$] per day when engaged on business of the Advisory Council] [in accordance with state law].

(g) The Advisory Council may consider rules and regulations as provided in Section 12 and any other matters related to the purposes of this Act, which may be submitted to it by the Commission; and may make recommendations to the Commission on its own initiative concerning the administration of this Act.

ALTERNATE IV

Section 3. Air Pollution Control Commission

(a) There is hereby created the Air Pollution Control Commission, hereinafter referred to as "the Commission." [3] The members of the Commission shall be the heads of the Departments of [Health, Commerce, Conservation and Agriculture], and [five] members appointed by the Governor [with the consent of the Senate]. Of the [five] members appointed by the Governor, [one] shall be a licensed physician knowledgeable in the health effects of air pollution; [one] shall be a professional engineer experienced in the field of air pollution control; [one] shall be representative of local and regional air pollution control agencies; [one] shall be a representative of industry, be employed by a manufacturing, power generating or fuels firm within the State, and be experienced in air pollution control; and [one] shall be chosen at large.

(b) The terms of the appointed members shall be four years except that of the initially appointed members, one shall serve for one year, one shall serve for two years, one shall serve for three years, and two shall serve for four years, as designated by the Governor at the time of appointment. Whenever a vacancy occurs, the Governor shall appoint a member for the remaining portion of the unexpired term created by the vacancy.

---

[3] The Commission may be established as an independent agency but could be placed within an existing state department for housekeeping purposes. In any event, it is important that statutory authority flow directly to the Commission and that it have independent powers.

(c) The Commission shall select its own chairman from among its members.

(d) The Commission shall hold at least four regular meetings each year and such additional meetings as the chairman deems desirable, at a place and time to be fixed by the chairman. Special meetings shall be called by the chairman upon written request of any [four] members. [Five] members shall constitute a quorum. The heads of the Departments of [Health, Commerce, Conservation and Agriculture] each may designate a principal deputy or assistant to act in his place and stead on the Commission.

(e) In accordance with the [state merit system law], the Commission shall appoint a Director of Air Pollution Control, hereinafter referred to as "the Director," who shall be the principal administrative officer of the Commission.

(f) The Commission may employ such personnel and consultants as may be necessary for the administration of this Act. Subject to any applicable restrictions contained in law, any department or agency of the State may from its available resources provide the Commission with personnel and services, with or without charge. The Commission may compensate such other agencies for services.

Section 4. Powers

In addition to any other powers conferred on it by law the [appropriate state agency] [4] shall have power to:

1. Adopt, amend and repeal rules and regulations implementing and consistent with this Act.

2. Hold hearings relating to any aspect of or matter in the administration of this Act, and in connection therewith, compel the attendance of witnesses and the production of evidence.

3. Issue such orders as may be necessary to effectuate the purposes of this Act and enforce the same by all appropriate administrative and judicial proceedings.

4. Require access to records relating to emissions which cause or contribute to air contamination.

5. Secure necessary scientific, technical, administrative and operational services, including laboratory facilities, by contract or otherwise.

6. Prepare and develop a comprehensive plan or plans for the prevention, abatement and control of air pollution in this State.

7. Encourage voluntary cooperation by persons and affected groups to achieve the purposes of this Act.

8. Encourage local units of government to handle air pollution problems within their respective jurisdictions and on a cooperative basis, and provide technical and consultative assistance therefor.

9. Encourage and conduct studies, investigations and research relating to air contamination and air pollution and their causes, effects, prevention, abatement and control.

10. Determine by means of field studies and sampling the degree of air contamination and air pollution in the State and the several parts thereof.

---

[4] Since the administrative organization of the agency is presented in alternative forms in Section 3, the term "[appropriate state agency]" will be used in the remainder of this Act.

11. Make a continuing study of the effects of the emission of air contaminants from motor vehicles on the quality of the outdoor atmosphere of this State and the several parts thereof, and make recommendations to appropriate public and private bodies with respect thereto.

12. Establish ambient air quality standards for the State as a whole or for any part thereof.

13. Collect and disseminate information and conduct educational and training programs relating to air contamination and air pollution.

14. Advise, consult, contract and cooperate with other agencies of the State, local governments, industries, other states, interstate or interlocal agencies, and the Federal Government, and with interested persons or groups.

15. Consult, upon request, with any person proposing to construct, install, or otherwise acquire an air contaminant source or device or system for the control thereof, concerning the efficacy of such device or system, or the air pollution problem which may be related to the source, device or system. Nothing in any such consultation shall be construed to relieve any person from compliance with this Act, rules and regulations in force pursuant thereto, or any other provision of law.

16. Accept, receive and administer grants or other funds or gifts from public and private agencies, including the Federal Government, for the purpose of carrying out any of the functions of this Act. Such funds received by the [appropriate state agency] pursuant to this Section shall be deposited in the State Treasury to the account of the [appropriate state agency].

SECTION 5. CLASSIFICATION AND REPORTING

(a) The [appropriate state agency], by rule or regulation, may classify air contaminant sources, which in its judgment may cause or contribute to air pollution, according to levels and types of emissions and other characteristics which relate to air pollution, and may require reporting for any such class or classes. Classifications made pursuant to this subsection may be for application to the State as a whole or to any designated area of the State, and shall be made with special reference to effects on health, economic and social factors, and physical effects on property.

(b) Any person operating or responsible for the operation of air contaminant sources of any class for which the rules and regulations of the [appropriate state agency] require reporting shall make reports containing information as may be required by the [appropriate state agency] concerning location, size and height of contaminant outlets, processes employed, fuels used and the nature and time periods or duration of emissions, and such other information as is relevant to air pollution and available or reasonably capable of being assembled.

SECTION 6. ADDITIONAL CONTAMINANT CONTROL
MEASURES

(a) The [appropriate state agency] may require that notice be given to it prior to the undertaking of the construction, installation or establishment of particular types or classes of new air contaminant sources specified in its rules and regulations. Within [fifteen] days of its receipt of such

notice, the [appropriate state agency] may require, as a condition precedent to the construction, installation or establishment of the air contaminant source or sources covered thereby, the submission of plans, specifications and such other information as it deems necessary in order to determine whether the proposed construction, installation or establishment
will be in accord with applicable rules and regulations in force pursuant
to this Act. If within [thirty] days of the receipt of plans, specifications or
other information required pursuant to this Section the [appropriate state
agency] determines that the proposed construction, installation or establishment will not be in accord with the requirements of this Act or applicable rules and regulations, it shall issue an order prohibiting the construction, installation or establishment of the air contaminant source or
sources. Failure of such an order to issue within the time prescribed herein
shall be deemed a determination that the construction, installation or
establishment may proceed: provided that it is in accordance with the
plans, specifications or other information, if any, required to be submitted.

(b) In addition to any other remedies available on account of the issuance of an order prohibiting construction, installation or establishment,
and prior to invoking any such remedies, the person or persons aggrieved
thereby shall, upon request in accordance with rules of the [appropriate
state agency], be entitled to a hearing on the order. Following such hearing, the order may be affirmed, modified or withdrawn.

(c) For the purposes of this Act, addition to or enlargement or replacement of an air contaminant source, or any major alteration therein,
shall be construed as construction, installation or establishment of a new
air contaminant source.

(d) Any features, machines and devices constituting parts of or called for by plans, specifications or other information submitted pursuant to
subsection (a) hereof shall be maintained in good working order.

(e) Nothing in this Section shall be construed to authorize the [ap-
propriate state agency] to require the use of machinery, devices or equipment from a particular supplier or produced by a particular manufacturer,
if the required performance standards may be met by machinery, devices
or equipment otherwise available.

(f) The absence or failure to issue a rule, regulation or order pursuant
to this Section shall not relieve any person from compliance with any
emission control requirements or with any other provision of law.

(g) The [appropriate state agency] by rule or regulation may prescribe and provide for the payment and collection of reasonable fees for the
review of plans and specifications required to be submitted pursuant to
this Section. No fee for a single review shall exceed [$].[5]

SECTION 7. INSPECTIONS

Any duly authorized officer, employee, or representative of the [ap-
propriate state agency] may enter and inspect any property, premise or
place on or at which an air contaminant source is located or is being con-
structed, installed or established at any reasonable time for the purpose of
ascertaining the state of compliance with this Act and rules and regulations in force pursuant thereto. No person shall refuse entry or access to

---

[5] Provision should be made either for the retention and use of fees by the [appropriate
state agency], or for their payment into an appropriate fund in the State Treasury.

any authorized representative of the [appropriate state agency] who requests entry for purposes of inspection, and who presents appropriate credentials; nor shall any person obstruct, hamper or interfere with any such inspection. If requested, the owner or operator of the premises shall receive a report setting forth all facts found which relate to compliance status.

SECTION 8. EMISSION CONTROL REQUIREMENTS

The [appropriate state agency] may establish such emission control requirements, by rule or regulation, as in its judgment may be necessary to prevent, abate, or control air pollution. Such requirements may be for the State as a whole or may vary from area to area, as may be appropriate to facilitate accomplishment of the purposes of this Act, and in order to take account of varying local conditions.

SECTION 9. ENFORCEMENT

(a) Whenever the [appropriate state agency] has reason to believe that a violation of any provision of this Act or rule or regulation pursuant thereto has occurred, it may cause written notice to be served upon the alleged violator or violators. The notice shall specify the provision of this Act or rule or regulation alleged to be violated, and the facts alleged to constitute a violation thereof, and may include an order that necessary corrective action be taken within a reasonable time. Any such order shall become final unless, no later than [ ] days after the date the notice and order are served, the person or persons named therein request in writing a hearing before the [appropriate state agency]. Upon such request, the [appropriate state agency] shall hold a hearing. In lieu of an order, the [appropriate state agency] may require that the alleged violator or violators appear before the [appropriate state agency] for a hearing at a time and place specified in the notice and answer the charges complained of, or the [appropriate state agency] may initiate action pursuant to Section 17 of this Act.

(b) If, after a hearing held pursuant to subsection (a) of this Section, the [appropriate state agency] finds that a violation or violations have occurred, it shall affirm or modify its order previously issued, or issue an appropriate order or orders for the prevention, abatement or control of the emissions involved or for the taking of such other corrective action as may be appropriate. If, after hearing on an order contained in a notice the [appropriate state agency] finds that no violation has occurred or is occurring, it shall rescind the order. Any order issued as part of a notice or after hearing may prescribe the date or dates by which the violation or violations shall cease and may prescribe timetables for necessary action in preventing, abating or controlling the emissions.

(c) Nothing in this Act shall prevent the [appropriate state agency] from making efforts to obtain voluntary compliance through warning, conference or any other appropriate means.

(d) In connection with any hearing held pursuant to this Section, the [appropriate state agency] shall have power and upon application by any party it shall have the duty to compel the attendance of witnesses and the production of evidence on behalf of all parties.

SECTION 10. EMERGENCY PROCEDURE

(a) Any other provisions of law to the contrary notwithstanding, if the Director finds that a generalized condition of air pollution exists and that it creates an emergency requiring immediate action to protect human health or safety, the Director, with the concurrence of the Governor, shall order persons causing or contributing to the air pollution to reduce or discontinue immediately the emission of air contaminants, and such order shall fix a place and time, not later than twenty-four hours thereafter, for a hearing to be held before the [appropriate state agency]. Not more than twenty-four hours after the commencement of such hearing, and without adjournment thereof, the [appropriate state agency] shall affirm, modify or set aside the order of the Director.

(b) In the absence of a generalized condition of air pollution of the type referred to in subsection (a), but if the Director finds that emissions from the operation of one or more air contaminant sources is causing imminent danger to human health or safety, he may order the person or persons responsible for the operation or operations in question to reduce or discontinue emissions immediately, without regard to the provisions of Section 9 of this Act. In such event, the requirements for hearing and affirmance, modification or setting aside of orders set forth in subsection (a) shall apply.

(c) Nothing in this Section shall be construed to limit any power which the Governor or any other officer may have to declare an emergency and act on the basis of such declaration, if such power is conferred by statute or constitutional provision, or inheres in the office.

SECTION 11. VARIANCES

(a) Any person who owns or is in control of any plant, building, structure, establishment, process or equipment may apply to the [appropriate state agency] for a variance from rules or regulations. The [appropriate state agency] may grant such variance, but only after public hearing on due notice, if it finds that:

1. The emissions occurring or proposed to occur do not endanger or tend to endanger human health or safety; and

2. Compliance with the rules or regulations from which variance is sought would produce serious hardship without equal or greater benefits to the public.

(b) No variance shall be granted pursuant to this Section until the [appropriate state agency] has considered the relative interests of the applicant, other owners of property likely to be affected by the discharges, and the general public.

(c) Any variance or renewal thereof shall be granted within the requirements of subsection (a) and for time periods and under conditions consistent with the reasons therefor, and within the following limitations:

1. If the variance is granted on the ground that there is no practicable means known or available for the adequate prevention, abatement or control of the air pollution involved, it shall be only until the necessary means for prevention, abatement or control become known and available, and subject to the taking of any substitute or alternate measures that the [appropriate state agency] may prescribe.

2. If the variance is granted on the ground that compliance with the particular requirement or requirements from which variance is sought will

necessitate the taking of measures which, because of their extent or cost, must be spread over a considerable period of time, it shall be for a period not to exceed such reasonable time as, in the view of the [appropriate state agency] is requisite for the taking of the necessary measures. A variance granted on the ground specified herein shall contain a timetable for the taking of action in an expeditious manner and shall be conditioned on adherence to such timetable.

3. If the variance is granted on the ground that it is justified to relieve or prevent hardship of a kind other than that provided for in items 1 and 2 of this subparagraph, it shall be for not more than [one] year.

(d) Any variance granted pursuant to this Section may be renewed on terms and conditions and for periods which would be appropriate on initial granting of a variance. If complaint is made to the [appropriate state agency] on account of the variance, no renewal thereof shall be granted, unless following public hearing on the complaint on due notice, the [appropriate state agency] finds that renewal is justified. No renewal shall be granted except on application therefor. Any such application shall be made at least [sixty] days prior to the expiration of the variance. Immediately upon receipt of an application for renewal the [appropriate state agency] shall give public notice of such application in accordance with rules and regulations of the [appropriate state agency].

(e) A variance or renewal shall not be a right of the applicant or holder thereof but shall be in the discretion of the [appropriate state agency]. However, any person adversely affected by a variance or renewal granted by the [appropriate state agency] may obtain judicial review thereof [in the manner provided by the State Administrative Procedure Act] [by a proceeding in the [   ] court]. Notwithstanding any provision of Section 12 of this Act, judicial review of the denial of a variance or denial of renewal thereof may be had only on the ground that the denial was arbitrary or capricious.

(f) Nothing in this Section and no variance or renewal granted pursuant hereto shall be construed to prevent or limit the application of the emergency provisions and procedures of Section 10 of this Act to any person or his property.

SECTION 12. HEARINGS AND JUDICIAL REVIEW

(a) No rule or regulation and no amendment or repeal thereof shall take effect except after public hearing on due notice [as provided in the State Administrative Procedure Act] [insert desired procedural details, if there is no applicable statute], and the Advisory Council has been afforded not less than [thirty] days, prior to publication of the proposed text, to comment thereon.[6]

(b) Nothing in this Section shall be construed to require a hearing prior to the issuance of an emergency order pursuant to Section 10 of this Act.

(c) Any person aggrieved by any order of the [appropriate state agency] may have judicial review thereof [in the manner provided by the State Administrative Procedure Act] [if there is no State Administrative Procedure Act, supply appropriate provisions for judicial review].

---

[6] If Section 3, Alternate II or IV, is selected as the form of organization for the air pollution control agency, this provision will not be appropriate.

SECTION 13. CONFIDENTIALITY OF RECORDS

Any records or other information furnished to or obtained by the [appropriate state agency] concerning one or more air contaminant sources, which records or information, as certified by the owner or operator, relate to production or sales figures or to processes or production unique to the owner or operator or which would tend to affect adversely the competitive position of such owner or operator, shall be only for the confidential use of the [appropriate state agency] in the administration of this Act, unless such owner or operator shall expressly agree to their publication or availability to the general public. Nothing herein shall be construed to prevent the use of such records or information by the [appropriate state agency] in compiling or publishing analyses or summaries relating to the general condition of the outdoor atmosphere: provided that such analyses or summaries do not identify any owner or operator or reveal any information otherwise confidential under this Section.

SECTION 14. LOCAL AIR POLLUTION CONTROL PROGRAMS

(a) Each municipality [with a population in excess of [ ]] [of [ ] class] and each county [with a population of [ ]] (excluding the population of municipalities in which a local air pollution control program has been established and approved as provided herein) shall, within [two] years from the date of enactment hereof, establish and thereafter administer within its jurisdiction an air pollution control program, which:

1. Provides by ordinance or local law for requirements compatible with, or stricter or more extensive than those imposed by Sections 8, 10 and 11 of this Act and regulations issued thereunder;

2. Provides for the enforcement of such requirements by appropriate administrative and judicial process;

3. Provides for administrative organization, staff, financial and other resources necessary to effectively and efficiently carry out its program; and

4. Is approved by the [appropriate state agency] as adequate to meet the requirements of this Act and any applicable rules and regulations pursuant thereto.

(b) Municipalities and counties, other than those so required under subsection (a) of this Section, may establish and administer air pollution control programs provided such programs meet the requirements of subsection (a) of this Section.

(c) Any municipality or county may administer all or part of its air pollution control program in cooperation with one or more municipalities or counties of this State or of other states provided that the requirements of the [State Interlocal Cooperation Act] [7] are met. Timely performance by or on behalf of a municipality or county pursuant to such cooperative undertaking shall be considered to be performance by the municipality or county for purposes of this Act.

(d) If the [appropriate state agency] finds that the location, charac-

---

[7] If the state has a statute providing for joint or cooperative exercise of local powers by two or more subdivisions within or without the State, make appropriate reference to it. Otherwise, include appropriate provisions for the establishment of joint air pollution control agencies or the establishment of air pollution control districts including two or more subdivisions and responsible to them.

ter or extent of particular concentrations of population, air contaminant sources, the geographic, topographic or meteorological considerations, or any combinations thereof, are such as to make impracticable the maintenance of appropriate levels of air quality without an areawide air pollution control program, the [appropriate state agency] may determine the boundaries within which such program is necessary and require it as the only acceptable alternative to direct State administration.

(e) 1. If a municipality or county required to establish or participate in an air pollution control program pursuant to subsections (a) or (d) of this Section fails to establish such program within the time required, or if the [appropriate state agency] has reason to believe that an air pollution control program in force pursuant to this Section is inadequate to prevent and control air pollution in the jurisdiction to which such program relates, or that such program is being administered in a manner inconsistent with the requirements of this Act, the [appropriate state agency] shall, on due notice, conduct a hearing on the matter.

2. If, after such hearing, the [appropriate state agency] determines that the municipality or county has failed to establish a required air pollution control program, or that such program is inadequate to prevent and control air pollution in the municipality, county, or municipalities or counties to which such program relates, or that such program is not accomplishing the purposes of this Act, it shall require that necessary corrective measures be taken within a reasonable period of time, not to exceed [   ].

3. If the municipality, county, or municipalities or counties fail to take such necessary corrective action within the time required, the [appropriate state agency] shall administer within such municipality, county, or municipalities or counties all of the regulatory provisions of this Act. Such air pollution control program shall supersede all municipal or county air pollution laws, regulations, ordinances and requirements in the affected jurisdiction. The cost of such administration shall be a charge on the municipality or county.

4. If the [appropriate state agency] finds that the control of a particular class of air contaminant source because of its complexity or magnitude is beyond the reasonable capability of the local air pollution control authorities or may be more efficiently and economically performed at the State level, it may assume and retain jurisdiction over that class of air contaminant source, but in such event no charge shall be assessed against the locality on account thereof. Classifications pursuant to this paragraph may be either on the basis of the nature of the sources involved or on the basis of their relationship to the size of the communities in which they are located.

(f) Any municipality or county in which the [appropriate state agency] administers its air pollution control program pursuant to subsection (e) of this Section may with the approval of the [appropriate state agency] establish or resume a municipal or county air pollution control program which meets the requirements of subsection (a) of this Section.

(g) Nothing in this Act shall be construed to supersede or oust the jurisdiction of any local air pollution control program in operation on the effective date of this Act: provided that within [two] years from such date any such program shall meet all requirements of this Act for a local air pollution control program. Any approval required from the [appropriate state agency] shall be deemed granted unless the [appropriate state agency] takes specific action to the contrary.

SECTION 15. STATE AND FEDERAL AID

(a) [Use as much of this section as necessary to establish a program of state aid for local air pollution control programs].

(b) Any local air pollution control program meeting the requirements of this Act and rules and regulations pursuant thereto shall be eligible for state aid in an amount equal to [30] per cent of the locally funded annual operating cost thereof. In the case of a joint, cooperative, or other areawide program established pursuant to Section 14 of this Act, such state aid may be for the entire program or, if the [appropriate state agency] finds that one or more elements of separately administered programs are being carried on jointly or cooperatively in such a way as materially to increase the efficiency or effectiveness thereof, it may aid the element or elements being carried on pursuant to the interlocal agreement. A joint, cooperative or other areawide program shall be entitled to state aid in the amount of [50] per cent of the locally funded annual operating cost thereof.

(c) Subdivisions of this State and interlocal air pollution control agencies established pursuant to this Act may make application for, receive, administer and expend any federal aid for the control of air pollution or the development and administration of programs related to air pollution control: provided that any such application is first submitted to and approved by the [appropriate state agency] shall approve any such application if it is consistent with this Act and any other applicable requirements of law.

SECTION 16. MOTOR VEHICLE POLLUTION

(a) As the state of knowledge and technology relating to the control of emissions from motor vehicles may permit or make appropriate, and in furtherance of the purposes of this Act, the [appropriate state agency] may provide by rules and regulations for the control of emissions from motor vehicles. Such rules and regulations may prescribe requirements for the installation and use of equipment designed to reduce or eliminate emissions and for the proper maintenance of such equipment and of vehicles. Any rules or regulations pursuant to this Section shall be consistent with provisions of federal law, if any, relating to control of emissions from the vehicles concerned. The [appropriate state agency] shall not require, as a condition precedent to the initial sale of a vehicle or vehicular equipment, the inspection, certification or other approval of any feature or equipment designed for the control of emissions from motor vehicles, if such feature or equipment has been certified, approved or otherwise authorized pursuant to federal law.

(b) Except as permitted or authorized by law, no person shall fail to maintain in good working order or remove, dismantle or otherwise cause to be inoperative any equipment or feature constituting an operational element of the air pollution control system or mechanism of a motor vehicle and required by rules or regulations of the [appropriate state agency] to be maintained in or on the vehicle. Any such failure to maintain in good working order or removal, dismantling or causing of inoperability shall subject the owner or operator to suspension or cancellation of the registration for the vehicle by the [state motor vehicle agency]. The vehicle shall not thereafter be eligible for registration until all parts and equipment constituting operational elements of the motor vehicle have been restored, replaced or repaired and are in good working order.

(c) The [appropriate state agency] shall consult with the [state motor vehicle agency] and furnish it with technical information, including testing techniques, standards and instructions for emission control features and equipment.

(d) When the [appropriate state agency] has issued rules and regulations requiring the maintenance of features or equipment in or on motor vehicles for the purpose of controlling emissions therefrom, no motor vehicle shall be issued an inspection sticker as required pursuant to [cite appropriate section of motor vehicle inspection law], unless all such required features or equipment have been inspected in accordance with the standards, testing techniques and instructions furnished by the [appropriate state agency] pursuant to subsection (b) hereof and has been found to meet those standards.

(e) The remedies and penalties provided in this Section shall apply to violations hereof, and no provision of Section 17 of this Act shall apply thereto.

(f) As used in this Section "motor vehicle" shall have the same meaning as in [cite appropriate section of state motor vehicle statute].

SECTION 17. PENALTIES

(a) Any person who violates any provision of this Act, or any rule or regulation in force pursuant thereto, other than Sections 13 and 16, shall be guilty of an offense and subject on account thereof to a fine of not to exceed [$1,000]. Each day of violation shall constitute a separate offense.

(b) Any person who willfully violates Section 13 of this Act shall be guilty of an offense and subject on account thereof to a fine of not to exceed [$1,000].

(c) Action pursuant to subsections (a) or (b) of this Section shall not be a bar to enforcement of this Act, rules and regulations in force pursuant thereto, and orders made pursuant to this Act by injunction or other appropriate remedy, and the [appropriate state agency] shall have power to institute and maintain in the name of this State any and all such enforcement proceedings.

(d) Nothing in this Act shall be construed to abridge, limit, impair, create, enlarge or otherwise affect substantively or procedurally the right of any person to damages or other relief on account of injury to persons or property and to maintain any action or other appropriate proceeding therefor.

SECTION 18. LIMITATIONS

Nothing in this Act shall be construed to:

1. Grant to the [appropriate state agency] any jurisdiction or authority with respect to air contamination existing solely within commercial and industrial plants, works or shops.

2. Affect the relations between employers and employees with respect to or arising out of any condition of air contamination or air pollution.

3. Supersede or limit the applicability of any law or ordinance relating to sanitation, industrial health or safety.

SECTION 19. EFFECTIVE DATE

[Insert effective date].